⌐AND⌐ ARGUMENT PERSUASION

SUSAN DAVIES

HEINEMANN
EDUCATIONAL

Heinemann Educational Publishers
Halley Court, Jordan Hill, Oxford OX2 8EJ
a division of Reed Educational & Professional Publishing Ltd

MELBOURNE   AUCKLAND   FLORENCE
PRAGUE   MADRID   ATHENS   SINGAPORE
TOKYO   SAO PAULO   CHICAGO   PORTSMOUTH (NH)
MEXICO   IBADAN   GABORONE   JOHANNESBURG
KAMPALA   NAIROBI

British Library Cataloguing in Publication Data
Davies, Susan *1957*
  Argument & Persuasion. - (English in action)
  I. Title
  428

ISBN: 0 435 10226 5

First published 1990
97 12 11 10 9

Cover design: Design Revolution, Brighton
Designed by Design Revolution, Brighton
Printed and bound in Great Britain by
The Bath Press, Bath

For Hannah, who keeps me smiling with
love and kisses.
Mum

Introduction

When teachers evaluate a coursebook they normally ask themselves a series of questions. The first one is always 'Can I afford it?' I hope that when you have read this introduction and perused the book you will decide that you can afford it and that you must have it.

Why do I need a resource book of this kind?

Argument and Persuasion provides you with ready-made resource material on a number of issues that pupils are interested in. The aim is to provide coursework material that would fulfil the requirement of GCSE criteria and latterly National Curriculum demands that pupils learn to select information, discuss it critically, and summarise and evaluate it effectively. As a teacher I felt that I did not always have the time to provide my pupils with the resource material they needed to complete this task well. I decided that I should set about providing resource material that would stand up to scrutiny, not just by the existing group of pupils I was teaching, but also by groups I would take in the following years. To quote the words of a colleague of mine uttered following his spending a month planning a literature scheme of work, 'You know what I will be doing in my literature lessons for the next ten years!' As English teachers we know the comment was far from the truth, though few would disagree that there is an element of common sense in the remark just the same. We do need material that we can use for a number of years that will not demand too much revising and I hope that this book will provide just that. Thus, the book covers a range of subjects that would interest a cross-section of pupils whose abilities and interests will by definition be different. Look at the contents list. Don't pupils show an interest in many of these issues? How many pupils might enjoy fishing, actually be vegetarian, or be opposed to people wearing fur coats? The biggest problem with discursive work is that it can focus on subjects that are altogether depressing. The inclusion of material on ghosts, the Loch Ness monster as well as the Yeti should help to dispel such a myth.

Why buy a book just for discursive work?

Discursive work provides pupils with problems for two reasons, Firstly, the pupil has to write or talk as an expert on the subject, something few of them can be without being provided with adequate resource material. Secondly, this type of discussion or writing needs a range of skills. Perhaps the most important of these skills is to read and evaluate the material in the right way. Pupils need to understand the power of the picture and more importantly still the power of language. The first chapter of the book aims to do this, using a variety of media. It both demonstrates to pupils the manipulative power of word and picture and shows them how they might use both in their own work. It can be used as introductory work before tackling the main units or as a reference tool during work on them. As a teacher constantly pressured by coursework demands I think it is important that any topic of work provides as much varied assignment material as possible. *Argument and Persuasion* therefore encourages pupils to write imaginatively and informationally and to discuss formally and informally. They can produce advertising campaigns, write reports, diaries, study poetry, prose and drama extracts and respond to them. They are encouraged to undertake a lot of small group discussion work and occasionally to mount a full-scale debate. The literary pieces can just as easily provide coursework for literature folders as for English and can thus be used for dual certificates syllabuses. The material and tasks are suited to all pupils and differentiation is by outcome.

Am I convinced?

To sum up *Argument and Persuasion* is a text book that provides a pupil with the means to develop discursive skills from informal discussion to authoritative essays. It portrays the way the media persuades the public to adopt a certain viewpoint, as well as teaching pupils via assignments to do just the same thing. The range of assignments prevents pupils becoming bored with a familiar kind of task. *Argument and Persuasion* is a book full of resource material intended to interest both the pupil and the teacher and I hope that you enjoy working with it as much as I enjoyed researching and writing it.

Contents

CHAPTER 1

Foundation skills

+

[WHO ARE THE PERSUADERS?]

The material in this book sets out to persuade you to adopt certain viewpoints. Everyone has at some time been influenced by an article, leaflet or advertisement they have read. We are only human after all. However, it is important that you realise you are being influenced and how this is being done.

ASSIGNMENT ❶

Look at the mass of material on pages 7 and 8.

ASSIGNMENT

In groups make a list of the people you think are responsible for each item on pages 7 and 8. Possible answers to this will be newspapers, political parties or societies who have a vested interest in a certain issue. Try to pinpoint exactly who is responsible for what.

Why is it necessary to know who has produced the material we read?

How does each article attract your attention?

Use the 'Help' section on page 9.

WOMEN

Teaching the sins of the flesh

Violet Johnstone on a campaign to remove meat from the schoolchild's curriculum

The steady growth in vegetarianism is being given a sudden boost with a campaign which is proving highly successful in schools. While more adults are turning to vegetarian diets for health reasons, their offspring are far m— —cely to be converted on — — of cruelty to animals. — your children have — me back asking for — s or chunky nut roasts — seen the video, *The*

Vegetarian World, which should get an Oscar for effective propaganda. Many children will feel an instant affinity with the little girl who says simply, "I'm a vegetarian because I love animals"; all will squirm at the sight of knives being plunged into the throats of chickens hanging helplessly upside down as they wait for slaughter.

Scream!, the School Campaign for Reaction Against Meat, is the new youth pressure group of the Vegetarian Society, which is sending information packs on the "real horrors of factory farming and abuse of animals" into schools, and offering to give talks and show a video on the subject. Emotive stuff.

Leaflets give vivid descriptions of fluffy chicks having the end of their beaks hacked off so that they will not peck each other to death as they grow, crammed together, in tiny cages, and of sows dragged back to the "rape rack" five days

after their piglets are weaned at two weeks. (It's unfortunate that the picture of the pig stall on one leaflet should be 13 years old.)

A small green booklet, *The A to Z of Vegetarianism*, has powerful messages for young people very open to persuasion. Under "H" for Health, children are told: "It has been proven that vegetarians suffer much less from heart disease, diabetes, bowel cancer and many other fatal illnesses. Under "S" for School Dinners, "Remember, it is your right to have vegetarian food at school and it should be provided".

(The evidence for vegetarians suffering fewer diseases is based solely on studies from religious groups such as the Seventh Day Adventists. So far no study among the general public can substantiate the Vegetarian Society's claims. For reasons that are not known, all religious sects seem to have low rates of certain diseases, irrespective of whether or not they eat meat and dairy products. No child has the "right" to vegetarian food at school, where meals are at the discretion of individual local education authorities.)

The video is aimed at children of 13 upwards, and the Society is making another for primary schools. "Children tend to be more sympathetic than adults," says Juliet Gellatley, the Society's Youth Education Officer, "They do things by gradual process. They'll give up meat, then fish, then leather shoes." It is natural that they then become vegan, she says,

At Bishop Heber High School, near Chester, Ms Gellatley "swayed many pupils", says Dr Paul Fenwick, the biology teacher. "The children were very distressed by the film they saw. The slaughter of animals didn't go down well." He admitted that no talk putting forward the other point of view was being planned.

It was the same at Davenport School in Stockport, where Ms Gellatley is giving four talks. "Nobody has approached us so we are not having a speaker 'from the other side', though it would be a

good idea - farmers are too busy, I suppose," says Eileen Howarth, home economics teacher.

The National Farmer's Union says its policy is to encourage farmers to give talks, but that it doesn't have a school programme as such. "If people don't want to eat meat you can't do anything about it," said the spokeswoman.

Other organisations produce good, balanced literature but are unwilling to get involved in any hard-hitting campaign. The Meat and Livestock Commission says firmly that it wouldn't adopt the same approach as the Vegetarian Society, but is successful in many school projects. For example, it will sponsor children who eat a school meal containing meat to the tune of 10p per meal for, say, a week and give the money to charity.

The Association of Agriculture maintains it just hasn't the funds to send speakers into schools. Common sense does prevail, it says; 75 per cent of teachers would recognise Scream! as propaganda.

However, with its school campaign the Vegetarian Society is bringing the issue of intensive farming to children's notice and it seems a shame that no one is putting forward the other side of this picture. Roger Ewbank of the Universities Federation for Animal Welfare, which aims to speak to students but does sometimes talk to sixth forms, says that many of the concerns are correct.

"But what is the alternative to battery birds if society wants eggs and poultry produced under hygienic conditions at prices it can afford to pay? The Ministry of Agriculture has a unit in Cleethorpes looking at aviary and perchary systems indoors, but where birds have a social life and can jump from perch to perch, and where there's an impression of living going on. But such units are more difficult to run."

He points out that there is a higher incidence of disease among free range birds.

Doesn't this make good school debating material?

e Vegetarian Society's school pack

THREE OUT OF FOUR BACK MERCY KILLING

by CHRIS MIHILL
Medical Correspondent

THREE out of four people are in favour of legalising mercy killing, a survey revealed yesterday.

Half of those questioned support euthanasia provided it is requested by a patient who is critically ill and in pain.

A further 23 per cent favour death on request regardless of the severity of the illness or pain.

Around a third of those who support euthanasia believe that relatives should be allowed to ask for it on behalf of a patient unable to communicate.

Mori interviewed 1,808 adults after being commissioned by two pressure groups opposed to euthanasia, Doctors Who Respect Human Life and the Human Rights Society.

The groups called the results "frightening" and "the start of the slippery slope towards the gas chambers".

Forty per cent of those questioned felt that if a patient had asked for euthanasia, a doctor should be obliged to carry it out.

- How can a picture attract your attention?
- Is a headline important?
- Look up the word **ambiguous** in a dictionary.
- Have you ever been attracted to an advertisement because of an ambiguous catch-phrase?
- What do you think a catch-phrase is?
- Why do you think it is called a catch-phrase?
- What does it try to do?

ASSIGNMENT 3

A school is full of advertisements promoting book-shops, holidays and so on. Many teachers have posters of some kind on their classroom walls. Make a survey of the material to be found on display in school. Does any of it set out to persuade you to buy something, go somewhere, or adopt a certain point of view? How does it attract your attention?

Is it visually attractive? Does it have an interesting slogan?

Make a list of things that are advertised in your town. Where are the advertisements placed?

How does advertising get into your home?

List ten advertisements that you have heard, seen or found in your home.

ASSIGNMENT 4

You should now have a long list of advertisements. For each advert make a note beside it of the following:

Where did you find it or hear it or see it?

Who is the advertisement aimed at? What age group of person does it set out to attract?

Does this affect where the advertisement is placed?

In what way does the advertisement set out to attract a certain age group?

ASSIGNMENT 5

Choose an advertisement that you think is very good. Describe what is being advertised and how the advertisement appeals to you. Try to explain why it does this and why you think it is a good advertisement.

- Is it funny?
- Is it clever in some way? Does it contain an amusing slogan?
- Is it very visual?
- Is it selling a product you like?
- Are you influenced by a famous person who is advertising the product?
- Are there any experts in the advertisement?
- Does it make special claims for the product?
- Does it appeal to your vanity or your desire to be like someone else? Does it promise success of some kind?
- Does it play on any fears a person may have?

They say life begins at forty.
Not so long ago, that's about when it ended.

Today, when someone dies in their forties, we all say how tragic it is that they should die so young.

And yet back in the last century it was common-place to be attending a funeral of a person in their forties.

The average life expectancy was, after all, just forty-two.

Of course, apart from poor hygiene and sanitation, there was no immunisation against polio, diphtheria, tetanus, mumps, measles, whooping cough or German measles.

No real treatment for tuberculosis, diabetes, kidney failure, high blood pressure, heart disease, ulcers, skin disease or asthma.

No antibiotics such as penicillin to fight infectious diseases.

And serious smallpox epidemics were frequent.

Nowadays we take it for granted that all these conditions can be treated.

Why animals are vital to research.

It is thanks. largely to the breakthroughs that have been made through research which requires animals, that most of us are able to live into our seventies.

Over the past fifty years, the medicines and vaccines that have been developed from such research, have saved the lives of over half a million infants and children in Britain alone.

Smallpox has been eradicated worldwide. And trials of malaria vaccine may also soon lead to the control of this lethal fever.

Although we can now treat many cancers, heart disease, rheumatism, arthritis, diabetes and asthma there is still a need for safer and better medicines.

And of course, diseases such as multiple sclerosis, cystic fibrosis, muscular dystrophy,

Two Mutes (hired mourners) 1901.

senile dementia and AIDS desperately need more research.

It's not just people who benefit.

Yet people aren't the only ones who benefit from medical science. Research on animals has led to many advances in veterinary practice.

Dogs can be protected against distemper, parvo virus, hepatitis and kidney disease.

Cats are immunised against enteritis and cat flu.

And more research is needed to solve numerous diseases which afflict farm animals.

Among those who supervise research on animals are qualified veterinary surgeons; they along with their colleagues care about the welfare of animals.

Though they care for animals, naturally they also care for people. That is why they use animals in research.

Animal rights or human ills?

Although millions of pounds are being spent to discover alternatives to using animals, few of the techniques developed can replace animals completely in the discovery and safety testing of new medicines.

Until we find an equally valid way of testing medicines for safety and efficiency, animals have to be used.

The ABPI believes that we do not have to choose between animal rights or human ills. With the right kind of approach, both can benefit.

The new legislation can improve the care and welfare of research animals, without hindering the advance of medicine.

Perhaps by the end of the century, with the help of medical research, people will then be saying something a little different.

That life begins at sixty?

abpi

The Association of the British Pharmaceutical Industry.

FACT AND OPINION

ASSIGNMENT ❶

Look up the words **fact** and **opinion** in a dictionary. Write them down. Study the following statements and decide which is a fact and which is an opinion.

> I think it will rain later.
> It rained yesterday.
> Fox hunting is a barbaric sport.
> Foxes kill chickens.
> Fishing is a popular sport and recreation.
> Fish don't feel pain. *
> Capital punishment has been abolished in this country.
> Restoring hanging will serve as a deterrent to criminals. *
> The number of violent crimes has increased since the abolition of the death penalty.
> It takes 40 mink pelts to make one fur coat.
> Smoking can damage your health.
> Smoking cigars is not as dangerous as smoking cigarettes.

Note the statements marked by the asterisk (*). Very often opinion is presented as fact. The two statements that are asterisked read as if they have their basis in fact. They are actually just opinions.

Imagine the different types of people who might use the statements written above. Try to take on the role of the weather man/woman, reading the first two statements out as part of a weather broadcast. If a person dressed in a white coat told you they were a scientist and said to you 'Fish don't feel pain' and an anti-angling supporter said 'Fish do feel pain' who would you believe? Why?

Are we influenced easily by people in authority, people we admire, people who are supposedly experts? Could this knowledge be useful to advertisers? Why?

ASSIGNMENT ❷

Study the advertisement from The Association of the British Pharmaceutical Industry (page 10) carefully.

ASSIGNMENT ❸

1 What is the advertisement about?

2 What is the advertiser trying to sell?

3 In your own words list five facts that the article contains.

4 In your own words list five opinions that the article contains.

5 Read the following sentences and explain whether they are facts, opinions or opinions presented as facts, and give reasons. Some sentences have been underlined to help you. They are underlined because they point to some information that has been left out and/or they contain statements that could be backed up with evidence.

It is thanks largely to the breakthroughs that have been made through research which requires animals, that most of us are able to live into our seventies.

Over the past fifty years, the medicines and vaccines that have been developed from such research, have saved the lives of over half a million infants and children in Britain alone.

Smallpox has been eradicated worldwide.

6 Who benefits from the research?

7 Why do you think it mentions the fact that animals as well as humans benefit from research? How might this influence a reader?

8 What is the purpose of the mutes in the advertisement? Would you have included them if you were the designer of this advertisement – if not suggest an alternative. Give reasons for your views.

9 How and in what way does the headline aim to attract the attention of the reader?

10 Explain how you feel about the importance of animal experiments after reading this and suggest ways in which the advertisement has tried to influence you. Has it succeeded? You should think about the style of the article and the tone it adopts. How do these set out to persuade you?

TRY TO REMEMBER THE DIFFERENCE BETWEEN A FACT AND AN OPINION.

THE USE OF LANGUAGE

ASSIGNMENT ①

As you read the article *Cats Tortured To Find Cure for Backache* jot down any words that you think are particularly powerful, *eg* words that may have an emotional effect on a person reading it. Compare the lists of words that you all have.

Words are very powerful. They have two meanings. The first is a dictionary meaning,
eg TORTURE: infliction of severe bodily pain, *eg* as a punishment or means of persuasion; physical or mental pain.

However, many words have an added meaning. Try this simple test. One by one members of the group are to tell each other what picture is conjured up in their mind by the word torture. Pretend that you are on a psychiatrist's couch and he has just said 'Torture'. What did you think of immediately?

What you have just done as a group is to find out what connotation the word torture has for each of you. A connotation is an added meaning that some words like torture can have. Many words have connotations attached to them. These connotations can be favourable or unfavourable.

What type of connotation is attached to the word torture?

CATS TORTURED TO FIND CURE FOR BACKACHE

Pets die in lab hell

THOUSANDS of pet cats are being tortured to death in horrific university experiments to find a cure for human backache.

The helpless creatures die screaming in harrowing agony - crippled, mutilated and brain damaged by a series of barbaric tests.

The sadistic, secret research is centred at the University of California in Los Angeles, home to some of America's brightest young brains.

The scandal is being ignored. Top officials of the US government which has ploughed millions of dollars into the hush-hush horror, even deny that the animals suffer any pain.

But The People can reveal exclusive today the full catalogue of cruelty inflicted by laboratory scientists.

We have obtained gruesome pictures of the cats' hell which will shock the world.

CRUSHED

Peaches is one pathetic victim . . . . . 15 months old and fully conscious but in the last throes of life.

His back is crushed and fur is shorn. A fearsome electrode has been drilled fully into his head. Five more are planted beneath the wounds crisscrossing his shaven skin.

He has just suffered twin blasts of hot air to the back and intense electric shocks to his paws and tail. He is in for 119 more.

They call it the "fear test." The current is recorded on an electronic graph as it passes through the cat's tortured nerve cells in his cage at UCLA 's spinal research unit.

Doctors monitored Peaches' reaction before and after he was given shocks - to check his heart rate, respiration and brain response.

Dynamo is another stomach churning sight.

The lovable white kitten had his back crushed with lead weights before electrodes and wires were embedded beneath his skin.

A thousand more like him will perish this year. Some are tiny kittens.

Others are fully grown tabbies which fetch £100 on a blooming black market.

A student's tip-off led Lifeforce, a leading anti-vivisection group, to carry out an eight-month undercover investigation.

The group's founder, Peter Hamilton, said:

'Crippled animals die agonising deaths from what amounts to slow, systematic torture.

The surgeons give them names like *Pegleg*.

Then they break their spinal cords and plant electrodes in their heads. Kittens are dying also from burst bladders.

They have been "spinalised" - that is medical jargon for it. It means the cats and kittens cannot empty their bladders.

Many are dying this way in excruciating pain.'

Scientists claim the experiments are vital in their quest to find a cure for back complaints.

But Mr Hamilton, 36 says most of the tests are unnecessary.

And Bill Dyer, president of the pressure group, Last Chance For Animals, told The People: "The link is never explained.

"The results of the tests have never been published."

Source: The People 12/7/87

ASSIGNMENT ❷

Re-write the headline of the article *Cats Tortured To Find Cure for Backache* and the first paragraph so as to avoid using emotive words at all. Then compare the original text with yours. Write briefly explaining the different attitude a reader might have to your article and the original. Explain what you think you have learned so far about the power of language.

ASSIGNMENT ❸

As a group discuss what words you can use to describe people. Make a list of favourable ones and unfavourable ones.

Write two descriptions of a close friend of yours.

Make one of them favourable and the other unfavourable. The descriptions should be identical except that one uses favourable language, the other unfavourable.
eg My friend is skinny and noisy.
   My friend is slim and talkative.

■   Make a list of favourable words that you would like to use and then the equivalent list of unfavourable words before you begin.

ASSIGNMENT ❹

Newspapers and advertisements make use of emotive language. Look for examples of this. Try to decide why emotive language is being used.

ASSIGNMENT ❺

Choose a well-known household product that is advertised frequently. Cut out and paste a picture of the product on to a blank sheet of paper and using emotive language write the blurb that an advertiser might suggest to go with the product.

ASSIGNMENT ❻

Look at the cartoon and estate agent's blurb on page 14.

ASSIGNMENT ❼

Write a true description of this cottage as it is portrayed in the cartoon.

ASSIGNMENT ❽

Make a list of the words and phrases that estate agents use to describe properties. Here are some examples to help you:
   well designed, ideal location, choice property, extensively modernised to the highest standard, rural location, magnificent views, compact, immaculate, prestigious, well-appointed, traditional style, within walking distance.

Look once more at the estate agent's description of the cottage and your own. Which is more likely to sell the cottage? Discuss as a group why estate agents use language in the way they do.

ASSIGNMENT ❾

Imagine that you were selling your home, or make up the details of a house/flat for this purpose. Write the complete estate agent's description.

This should include the type of home for sale, location, specific attractions of the area and room sizes.

Indicate particular features of each room that you would wish to emphasise.

- Before you attempt this work go to an estate agent's and ask for an old property sheet. This will help you with the layout.

Twill Du Cottage

A delightful traditional type cottage.
In need of some renovation but retaining a wealth of charm and character bounded by a small stream. Ideally situated within 5 minutes motoring distance of the M4 and within walking distance of the local village
Capel Dewi.

ASSIGNMENT 10

Imagine that you are a teacher. Write your own end of year report as accurately as possible. Use the language that a teacher would use to write the report.

ASSIGNMENT 11

Design an advertisement to sell your school. Think of an unusual caption you could use in the advertisement.

- Estate agents have a language that they use to describe properties. Teachers have a special language that they use when they are writing reports. Certain words and phrases that are used by a profession in this way can be grouped together. A special term is used to describe these groups of words and phrases and the word is REGISTER. Other professions also have registers peculiar to them – can you think of any?
- Remember that if you are asked to write as if you are a teacher, estate agent and so on, then you must adopt the REGISTER of that profession.
- The layout of a document may also be important. Make sure that you adopt a layout that is suitable to the task you are undertaking.

[HEADLINES]

ASSIGNMENT ❶

Read the following headlines.

Smoking yob extinguished by heroine of the 8.57

Nessie: Sonar and yet so far

AN ABOMINABLE SAGA UNFOLDS

ASSIGNMENT ❷

Study the headlines above and try to decide how they aim to attract the attention of a reader.

ASSIGNMENT ❸

Read the following outlines to three stories and decide on a suitable eye-catching headline for each.

YESTERDAY in the Himalayas, Chris Bonington veteran explorer came face to face with the Abominable Snowman. He has pictures of himself and the Snowman drinking tea together. *Date, April 1st, 1990.*

FOUR dogs have been stolen from an animal research laboratory. It is believed the Animal Freedom Fighters were responsible. The dogs were being successfully treated for cancer and their loss could put back this research at least 10 years unless they are safely recovered.

A BILL passed in parliament today has banned all smoking in public places. An on the spot fine of £5 will be payable. All collected fines are to be used to bolster National Health Service funds. Much National Health money is used to treat people with smoking related illnesses.

[WRITING A NEWSPAPER ARTICLE]

ASSIGNMENT ①

Look at the layout of the newspaper article below. Note carefully the type of information that is found there. The date, numbers of papers sold each day, competition news, details about stories within the paper might all be found on the front page along with an eye-catching front page story. Look care-

fully at how the story attracts your attention and then look at the style of writing. Write a page explaining how this story sets out to attract your attention. Think about the language used and the style adopted by the writer. Explain whether you think it is a good piece of journalism or not.

Read and discuss the help section on page 17 before you begin your individual writing.

NEWSPAPER OF THE YEAR

TUESDAY, SEPTEMBER 27, ✱✱✱ **DAILY SALE 574,282** (Week ending Sept 10) **20p** (Republic of Ireland 30p)

Ben Johnson caught taking steroids

STRIPPED OF GOLD

From CHRIS BOFFEY in Seoul

BEN JOHNSON, THE WORLD'S FASTEST MAN, SENSATIONALLY LOST HIS OLYMPIC GOLD MEDAL LAST NIGHT AFTER FAILING A DRUGS TEST.

Games president Juan Samaranch said last night: "This is a sad day for the Olympics. Johnson has been found taking drugs.

"I understand it is steroids. There is no other option but to strip him of his medal."

Johnson, 27, beat American Carl Lewis in the fastest ever time of 9.79 seconds on Saturday. Traces of anabolic steroids were found in a routine urine test afterwards.

Lewis will now be awarded the gold and Britain's third-place Linford Christie will get the silver medal.

Johnson's business manager Larry Hiederbrech said: "I cannot say anything now I am afraid I am gonna have to break some news to you guys later."

Later it was revealed that Johnson will appeal claiming the urine sample was mishandled.

But he is likely to be flown home immediately the decision is confirmed.

Astonishing

During last week's heats, Johnson has shown indifferent from, but he showed an astonishing burst of speed in the final.

After the 1987 world championships in Rome, when Johnson beat Lewis, the American made statements about runners taking drugs.

And after Saturday's final, Lewis said: "Ben wasn't the same person on Friday. That race was shocking. I don't know how he does it. Maybe he uses a hypnotist or something."

**A DRUGS SHOCK:
Back Page**

Nine mini-jeeps in death probe

by Kevin Eason

Thousands of jeep owners were urged last night to drive with special care after a roll-over accident during a government safety test.

The warning came after Transport Minister Peter Bottomley ordered tests on nine types of jeep amid growing concern over two Suzuki models highlighted Turn to page 2

TV BOOZE AD THAT BREAKS ALL THE RULES

by Nigel Bunyan and Jane Gordon

A sexy new Babycham commercial breaks almost all the latest guidelines designed to curb drink-related violence, TODAY can reveal.

Under a tough new code of practice, introduced yesterday by the Independent Broadcasting Authority, advertising agencies are warned not to employ people under 25 in drinks ads and banned from using personalities likely to appeal to young people.

But the new Babycham commercial due to be screened next week, violates the letter and spirit of the code.

Its heroine, a dull secretary called Jane, undergoes a complete transformation when Turn to page 2

22. Cartoons and Stars 23 City 24, 25 and 26. Sport starts 29

Source: Today 30/9/88.

- What do you think of the headline?
- Is it eye-catching?
- How does it relate to the article itself?
- Do you think you would be attracted to buy the paper having read this headline? Why?
- Can you think of an alternative headline?
- What information is contained in the first paragraph?
- Why is the main information of the story contained in this first paragraph?
- Could it encourage you to want to read further and get to the 'juicy bits' of the story?
- Does it tell you a lot about the substance of the story?
- What information is given later?
- Are pictures used?
- Is there anything unusual about the language?
- Could you take out any words that are unnecessary?
- How many?
- Would you say journalists use a few words to describe a lot?
- What style of writing do journalists use?
- Do they write just to give you the basic information necessary?
- Have you noticed anything about the layout of this story?
- How are newspaper articles generally set out?
- Is there a pattern here that you could follow?

ASSIGNMENT ②

From your analysis of the *Today* article, devise a list of rules that you could follow when writing a newspaper article that will ensure you always write one well.

ASSIGNMENT ③

It is important when you are writing a newspaper article that you aim to attract the attention of the reader. Imagine that you are writing the front page headline story. Choose one of the outlines on page 15 and write a full story to accompany it. You will have to use your imagination to write it.

- Remember the rules you made for yourself in assignment 2.

[THE POWER OF THE PICTURE]

Many advertisements are visual. This is also true of the front page of many leaflets. This page aims to make you realise how effective pictures really are. Remember there is *more* to a picture than meets the eye.

It takes up to 40 dumb animals to make a fur coat.

But only one to wear

LYNX
Fighting the fur trade
P O Box 509 Dunmow, Essex Tel 037

If you don't want animals gassed, electrocuted, trapped or strangled, don't buy a fur coat.

A S S I G N M E N T ❶

Study the poster carefully.

A S S I G N M E N T ❷

As a group discuss how the poster aims to catch your attention. Write a paragraph explaining what it is about and why you find it eye-catching. How has the artist set out to affect you emotionally?

- What impression do you get of the woman?
- How effective is the caption?
- How effective is the trail of blood?
- Why do you think it was included?

ASSIGNMENT ③

Look at the three pictures below. Decide which would be most effective for the front of an anti-nuclear arms leaflet. Explain with reasons what you think of each picture and why you chose the one you did.

ASSIGNMENT ④

Make an effort to look at as many advertisements as possible and choose some that aim to attract attention with their use of pictures.

- You might be asked how effective a photograph is. Ask yourself the following questions.
- What do the picture or pictures depict?
- If the picture/s are used with a passage – How do they relate to the passage?
- Why are the photographs there?
- Do they emphasise anything being said in an article?
- How do they attract the attention of the reader?
- How do they affect the reader? *ie* How do they affect you?

LETTERS, REPORTS AND ESSAYS

In the course of the assessment work you may be expected to write letters, reports and essays. In each the style and layout will differ.
Look at the layout of the following.

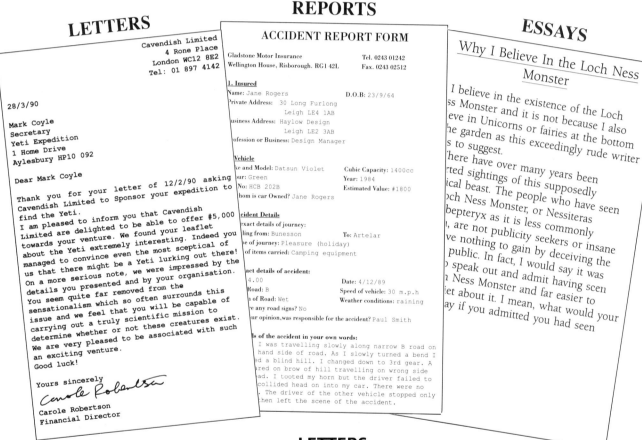

LETTERS

The style of a letter will depend on the purpose of the letter and who you are writing to. In discursive work most letters are of a formal nature. The language you use is dictated by this.

ASSIGNMENT ①

Imagine that you are writing a letter to the newspaper which printed the article *Cats Tortured to Find Cure for Backache* (page 12).
Read this article quickly. Imagine that you wished to complain about it. Your letter should be structured as follows.
Paragraph 1 This should explain your reason for writing. It is always brief and to the point.

Paragraph 2 This should identify why you are complaining. This is the most important part of the letter. It explains in detail why you object to the article. Is it the subject matter? The bias? The use of such emotive language? The explicit use of photographs of a disturbing nature?
Paragraph 3 This should sum up your overall attitude and indicate any action you intend to take if this is possible. Formal letters always end with 'Yours faithfully'.

Letters need careful planning and you should follow the pattern suggested to help you. This may vary slightly depending on the nature, circumstance and reasons for your correspondence.

REPORTS

Reports are usually written in order to give information in as factual and formal a fashion as possible.

ASSIGNMENT ②

Reports are written by a variety of people for a variety of reasons. Make a list of the people who would write reports and try to assess why the reports would be written.

ASSIGNMENT ③

Imagine that you have arrived late for school. On the way your bus was delayed because a cat got stuck up a tree and the rescuing fire engine blocked the road. You were the only school pupil on the bus. Then when you finally got to the bus station to walk the last half mile an old lady fell and you had to ring for an ambulance and wait for it to arrive. Finally, you manage to walk within 100 yards of the school gate when a small child comes up to you crying and says he is lost. You manage to take him home to his house but you are now two hours late and have to report to the headteacher and explain.

Write or tape the conversation that you would have with the headteacher of your school.

Write or tape the conversation you would have with a friend explaining why you are late.

ASSIGNMENT ④

As a group study the two conversations that you have written or taped.

How do they differ?
How are they similar?

Is one more formal than the other?
Should one be more formal than the other?
Why is this?
Has the language you have used varied?
Why is this?
Pick out words that you think are formal.
Pick out words that are informal in your conversations.

Reports are always written using formal language. They should actually look realistic. Not only should reports look formal but often they should adopt the style of language used by a certain group of people. Think about your school reports and the language that teachers use when writing them. The answers to the following questions will give you some more words that should be familiar to you and remind you of the type of language used by particular groups of people.

What name is given by the police to the place where an incident occurred?
What is the person who saw a crime called?
What does M.O. mean?
How is time denoted in reports? Do reports say 22.00 hours or 10 o'clock?

The language we use for specific occasions is very important. We are always influenced by the audience we are communicating with and the nature of the communication.

ASSIGNMENT ⑤

Read the poem *Incendiary*.

This poem is based on an actual happening. The boy who set fire to the haystacks and barn was an inmate of a home for maladjusted children in Kent. The boy was illegitimate, had come from an appalling foster home where he had been ill-treated and had never been shown a flicker of normal human affection.

INCENDIARY

That one small boy with a face like pallid cheese
And burnt-out little eyes could make a blaze
As brazen fierce and huge, as red and gold
And zany yellow as the one that spoiled
Three thousand guineas' worth of property
And crops at Godwin's farm on Saturday
Is frightening – as fact and metaphor:
An ordinary match intended for
The lighting of a pipe or kitchen fire
Misused may set a whole menagerie
Of flame-fanged tigers roaring hungrily
And frightening too, that one small boy
should set
The sky on fire and choke the stars to heat
Such skinny limbs and such a little heart
Which would have been content with one
warm kiss
Had there been anyone to offer this

VERNON SCANNELL

ASSIGNMENT 6

The following questions will help you understand the poem.

1 What had the boy in the poem done?

2 How much damage had been caused?

3 How is the boy described in the poem? Look at all the words that describe the boy. Jot down the words and phrases that are used.

4 What picture does the poet create of the boy?

5 What does the phrase 'a face like pallid cheese' mean?

6 Why are the boys' eyes described as 'burnt out'?

7 How did the fire start?

8 Look at the description of the fire. What impression do you get of the fire?

9 Can you pick out a metaphor that is used to describe it?

10 Why is the sky described as being 'on fire'?

11 What do the last three lines tell you about the boy and his home circumstances?

12 How do you feel about the little boy? Do you feel sorry for him?

Write the report that a police officer would complete having been at the scene of the fire.

Write a report that a social worker might give of this boy.

Write a newspaper article about the blaze.
When you have finished the three pieces look at the different layouts for each and the different styles of writing used.

ESSAYS

Writing a discursive essay is the most difficult task you will be faced with. This is because you have to argue your point of view and use material to substantiate why you feel this way.

ASSIGNMENT 7

The first thing you have to do is decide what the question is asking you. For instance, imagine that you are given the following question.

If you had the opportunity to make changes in your school what would you alter and why?

The essay question asks you two things – decide what they are.

ASSIGNMENT 8

Good essays develop from good essay plans. Now spend ten minutes deciding what changes you would make and give reasons each time.

Now ask yourself the following questions.
What structure will you use for your essay?
Will you suggest all the changes you wish to make and then give reasons; or will you suggest a change and follow it immediately with the reason?
What changes naturally go together and could be part of the same paragraph?
Will you start with major changes you propose and finish with minor ones or vice versa?

Decide how you will introduce your essay. All essays of this kind need an introductory paragraph.

Now think about how you might finish an essay of this kind. Every essay needs a concluding paragraph. This sums up in a few words the main ideas put forward in the essay.

Now you are ready to write a really well planned discursive essay.

SONGS AND POEMS

Poems and songs are often used as a way of getting across a powerful message to a large audience. The writer uses them to express how he/she feels about a certain subject.

CHILDREN'S CRUSADE

Young men, soldiers, nineteen fourteen
Marching through countries they'd never seen
Virgins with rifles, a game of charades
All for a children's crusade

Pawns in the game are not victims of chance
Strewn on the fields of Belgium and France
Poppies for young men, death's bitter trade
All of those young lives betrayed

The children of England would never be slaves
They're trapped on the wire and dying in
waves
The flower of England face down in the mud
And stained in the blood of a whole generation

Corpulent generals safe behind lines
History's lessons drowned in red wine
Poppies for young men, death's bitter trade
All of those young lives betrayed
All for a children's crusade

The children of England would never be slaves
They're trapped on the wire and dying in
waves
The flower of England face down in the mud
And stained in the blood of a whole generation

Midnight in Soho Nineteen Eighty Four
Fixing in doorways, opium slaves
Poppies for young men, such bitter trade
All of those young lives betrayed
All for a children's crusade

STING

THE SONG OF THE WHALE

Heaving mountain in the sea,
Whale, I heard you
Grieving.

Great whale, crying for your life,
Crying for your kind, I knew
How we would use
Your dying:

Lipstick for our painted faces,
Polish for your shoes.

Tumbling mountain in the sea,
Whale, I heard you
Calling.

Bird high notes, keening, soaring:
At their edge a tiny drum
Like a heartbeat.

We would make you
Dumb

In the forest of the sea,
Whale, I heard you
Singing,

Singing to your own kind,
We'll never let you be,
Instead of life we choose

Lipstick for our painted faces,
Polish for our shoes.

KIT WRIGHT

ASSIGNMENT 1

Often poems have a theme. They can have more than one. A theme is really the subject of the poem. Try to decide what the theme is in each of the pieces opposite. Is there a message in either that could be a hint as to the poem's theme? In a sentence or two write down what you think each is about.

ASSIGNMENT 2

One of the pieces opposite is a poem; the other the lyrics to a song. Can you tell which is which by just looking at them? What do songs usually have that poems often lack? Answer the following questions on *Song of the Whale*. They should help you understand what it is about.

1 How is the whale described?

2 Is the *Song of the Whale* happy or sad?

3 Why are the lines 'Lipstick for our painted faces/ Polish for our shoes' repeated by the writer?

4 What does the verse that begins *Bird high notes* describe?

5 How does the poet feel about the whale? How do you know this?

6 How do you feel about the plight of whales?

7 What do you think of the piece?

8 Is it written in a special way?

9 Writers of songs/poems have to use words carefully. They use one or two words where a story writer can use many. What words or phrases in this poem strike you as being carefully chosen?

10 Is the title important as a clue to the meaning?

ASSIGNMENT 3

Write about a page explaining what *Song of the Whale* is about. Base your ideas on your answers above and don't forget to explain how you felt about it.

ASSIGNMENT 4

Write a poem on an issue you feel strongly about.

- Try to decide what you feel strongly about.
- What do you want to say about it?
- Write down ten important statements to do with this.
- Try to decide on a structure for your poem. (A structure is the shape you wish to make it.)
- Then try to fit the words to this pattern. It will take time.

ASSIGNMENT 5

Look at *The Children's Crusade*. Decide what it is about and make up ten questions that would help someone understand it.

Could you always ask yourself basic questions about poems and songs? Would this help you to understand them?

CHAPTER 2

smoking and you!

For a long time we have been hearing that smoking damages health. However, recently attention has focused not on the smokers but on the non smokers who come into contact with them and breathe in their smoke. These people are called PASSIVE SMOKERS. Doctors would have us believe that this too is dangerous. Read the information that follows carefully. Weigh up both sides of the argument from the smoker and non smoker and then decide how you feel. Remember that it is *your* opinion that counts. When you have reached a decision you must be able to say why you have arrived at that decision. You must be able to say. 'I feel as I do because . . .' and then you should be able to give a list of reasons. As you read the information think carefully about who is telling you this. Are they in favour of smoking or against it? Does this matter? Why should this matter? Remember what was said about bias in *Foundation Skills*, page 11.

SHUT SMOKERS AWAY IN CORNER BY THEMSELVES

by KATE MANN

SMOKERS should be completely segregated in offices, factories, pubs and restaurants, says a new Government report.

Top scientists warn that drastic action is needed because non-smokers may face a 30 percent higher risk of lung cancer simply by breathing in other people's smoke.

They believe passive smoking may be responsible for "several hundred out of the current annual total of 40,000 lung cancer deaths in the UK".

The report, to be published later this week by the Department of Health, also warns that exposure to other people's smoke during pregnancy is linked to babies being born underweight.

"In two studies there was 24 grammes difference in birthweight between exposed and unexposed women," it says.

Smoking by parents may also increase the frequency and severity of childhood respiratory illnesses.

Harmful

The independent scientific committee chaired by Sir Peter Frogatt says improved ventilation, or the mixing of smoking and non-smoking areas within the same enclosed space is not enough to guard against the dangers.

It recommends that "consideration should be given to ways of ensuring that in the work and leisure environments, in public transport and in other public enclosed spaces, smokers can be segregated from non-smokers".

Mr David Simpson, head of the anti-smoking group ASH, welcomed the report.

He said: "This will end any debate about whether passive smoking is harmful — it is."

Protect

He said ASH was contacting environmental health officers asking them to consider prosecuting employers who failed to protect staff against other people's smoke.

But the Tobacco Advisory Council hit back: "There is a lack of consensus among scientists worldwide on this issue.

"The committee's interpretation must therefore be based on assumption and opinion rather than fact."

Source: Today 23/3/88

Courtesy of: Spence Herschberger, Health Edco Inc.

Smokers' campaigner fights to keep 'liberty and balance'

by John Neale

SMOKERS must have the right to smoke - that is the message being spread in the Channel Islands by Stephen Eyres, director of Forest, the Freedom Organisation for the Right to Enjoy Smoking Tobacco.

Forest sprang to prominence, locally with its vehement opposition to Air UK's 'Fresh Approach' no-smoking experiment on Channel Island flights.

Mr Eyres has been on a whistle-stop tour of Jersey and Guernsey, spreading his message.

Forest want to 'balance the debate and pressures about smoking. For too long, the anti-smoking lobby has had an unchallenged access to the media and nobody has defended the rights of people to be smokers - least of all, the tobacco industry', he says.

The organisation was formed in 1979, to put the case for the right of adults to make up their own minds to be smokers, and to have, in public places, areas where people can smoke as well as having no-smoking areas.

Mr Eyres says that one has got to 'have a lot of commonsense' on the question of smoking in public places. They would not press for smoking areas in places such as theatres, where the performers could be affected, and on small aircraft such as Aurigny's Trislanders 'it would be absolute nonsense' because it would be impossible to segregate the smokers from the non-smokers.

He feels that Air UK's claim that their planes are too small for effective segregation cannot be supported, especially on their larger Fokker aircraft.

Mr Eyres admits that they have no qualms about going to the big five tobacco companies for finance.

'The thing is that we are defending the rights of the tobacco industry's customers, and in addition to the industry funding things like... cricket matches and snooker tournaments and opera perfor-

mances, they also have a duty to defend the rights of their customers to continue buying their product,' he says.

Mr Eyres argues that it has not been established 'beyond doubt' that secondary smoke damages the non-smoker inhaling it, although it can be annoying.

'To go around saying that 200 or 2,000 non-smokers in Britain are dying of lung cancer caused by smokers hasn't been established.'

Mr Eyres, who says that he only 'occasionally' smokes a cigar after a meal and has never enjoyed nicotine, has taken up Forest's cause for 'liberty'.

'Liberty and balance, certainly.'

He has seen how much more extreme the anti-smoking campaign has become and feels the need to balance that.

'Now it's the right of 17m people in Great Britain to be smokers of cigarettes, cigars and pipes without discrimination, harrassment or social leper treatment.' he says.

'If Air UK, which is a private company, want to have a smoke-free enterprise, that's up to them. But equally, we have a duty to point out to smokers, operations in competition to Air UK, which are friendly to smokers. The key is competition.'

He denies that he is wasting his members' - of which there are 80 in the Channel Islands - funds on advertising 'against' Air UK because a Harris poll has shown that the majority of people want separate areas for smokers and non-smokers on planes and not a total ban.

'If non-smokers and anti-smokers want to flock to Air UK, that's fine by me because that's freedom of choice. But equally, we want to make sure that people who want to smoke and enjoy smoking while flying have a choice of an alternative, and our campaign is providing that information,' he says.

Source: Guernsey Evening Press

ASSIGNMENT 1

Study the information in the article titled *Smokers' Campaigner Fights to Keep Liberty and Balance* and in *Shut Smokers Away in Corner by Themselves*.

On a clean sheet of paper draw two columns. Head one **smoking** and the other **non smoking**. Make a list of reasons given in these articles why people should be allowed to continue smoking in public places under the smoking column and why they should not under the other column.

ASSIGNMENT 2

Can you think of any reasons to add to each column? Here are some suggestions:

Smoking is said to be unsociable. Can you think why?
What happens to your clothes when you are in the company of a smoker?
Does it affect you in any other ways?
How many people work in the tobacco industry?
How much is spent on advertising sponsorship?
How much does the Government receive from excise duty on cigarettes?

Compare your list with that of your friends in your group. Do you agree or disagree with their reasons? Add any you agree with to your columns.

LARRY'S **SMOKELESS ZONES**

Source: Punch.

ASSIGNMENT 3

Look carefully at the cartoons. Discuss in your groups what point you think the cartoonist is trying to make in each one.

ASSIGNMENT 4

It is **National No Smoking Day**. Design an advert for ASH (Action on Smoking and Health) advertising this and encouraging people to give up smoking and design an advert for FOREST (The Freedom Organisation for the Right to Enjoy Smoking Tobacco) encouraging smokers to stand up for their right to enjoy their habit and encouraging them to ignore National No Smoking Day!

- Remember adverts are eye-catching. They attract your attention by being visually good, or having a clever slogan that makes you think about what is being said, or they use language that encourages you to be swayed towards their product or way of thinking.

ASSIGNMENT ⑤

Read the article *Smoking Yob Extinguished By Heroine of the 8.57*.

Imagine that you are either the *heroine* or the *smoking yob*. Due to the coverage given to the incident by the media you have both been invited to talk to an audience about the incident and to give your views on the subject of smoking. Prepare the talk that you may wish to give, supporting your actions in this incident. Much of what you have written on your two-column sheet should help you here.

Smoking yob extinguished by heroine of the 8.57

IT WAS the sort of confrontation that often happens in British Rail's non-smoking compartments.

A scruffily dressed teenager slouches in and lights up a cigarette in defiance of the signs and everyone else's wishes and health.

The non-smokers usually suffer in silence — but the yob who tried it on the 8.57 pm to Chingford more than met his match.

At first he ignored the middle-aged woman who politely asked him to put out the cigarette.

by IAN FLETCHER

As the other commuters buried their heads deeper in their newspapers, she repeated the request.

The sneering yob's only response was to light up two more cigarettes and deliberately blow smoke from all three into her face.

In the best British tradition, the other passengers kept on pretending nothing was happening.

But the woman was made of sterner stuff.

She calmly picked up the compartment's fire extinguisher and put out all three cigarettes with a well-aimed jet that left the disbelieving teenager soaking wet from head to foot.

The other passengers broke into cheers — and finally joined the action, holding down the furious smoker as he tried to attack the woman.

One said: "We couldn't believe it when she blasted him with the extinguisher, but he certainly had it coming.

"Usually people do not react when something like this happens. You have to admire her guts."

No-one knows who the woman is, only that she left the train from London's Liverpool Street at Walthamstow.

British Rail said: "We can understand people getting annoyed but taking the law into their own hands is not the answer. This lady should have called the guard, who can report smokers to British Transport police. Offenders can be fined up to £50."

Source: Today 29/9/88

ASSIGNMENT ⑥

Look at the article *Fags Dragged into Court*.

In your own words explain what the article is about. What does it say about the people who are claiming damages from the tobacco companies? What types of health problems have they got? What does it have to say about the legal position of the passive smoker? What could they do?

Your summary should be about 300 – 400 words long. It could be used as an informational piece of writing to go in your folders along with the adverts you designed earlier.

Derek Morgan blows away the smoke on claims against tobacco firms

Fags dragged into court

THERE is no smoke these days without the hiring and firing of lawyers. Smoking litigation is about to become a major health issue in the United Kingdom.

The flames have been fanned by a recent American court case between the Liggett Group, manufacturers of Chesterfield cigarettes, and Tony Cipollone. He sued Liggett on his own behalf and that of his late wife Rose, who died (aged 58) of lung cancer in 1984. In late June, legal history was made when the New Jersey jury ordered Liggett to pay Cipollone $400,000 damages (about £238,000) for contributing to Rose's death. Liggett is to appeal.

This is the first time, after more than 300 cases brought against tobacco companies since the mid-fifties, that damages have been awarded.

Lawyers and pressure groups in Britain have followed the Cipollone case with interest. John Dean, a 33-year-old man from Northern Ireland with Beurger's disease, has become the first smoker to be awarded legal aid for a case against Imperial Tobacco. He claims that having smoked since the age of 10, cigarettes are directly responsible for his condition.

Beurger's disease, which affects the arteries, is believed to be caused by smoking. It is responsible for most of the 2,000 leg amputations performed in the UK each year. Dean's prognosis has improved since he stopped smoking, but he still does not know whether or not he will lose both his legs.

Andrew McFarlane, a personal injury specialist in Merseyside, has two more smoking cases in hand: one involving a toe amputation; the other, loss of the lower part of a leg. In a normal personal injury, damages against a defendant found fully liable could amount to over £40,000. McFarlane hopes to press at least one of these cases for aggravated damages.

The basis of the claims against the tobacco companies is twofold. Smokers allege that the companies' sale of their products warrants the safety of cigarettes and they claim the companies knew, or should have known, of the health risks of smoking and should either have ceased manufacture altogether or given more explicit and forceful warnings.

In the Cippolone case, the jury was shown adverts saying "L&M Filters are Just What the Doctor Ordered".

A senior lawyer in Britain has encouraged the anti-smoking group, Ash, to feel optimistic about the three cases pending in the UK. It has also been suggested that a non-smoker obliged to inhale second-hand smoke would be entitled to use reasonable force to oblige the smoker to stub out.

The smoker may be criminally assaulting the non-smoker, in which case the passive smoker could resort to self-defence. Some lawyers have doubted this claim.

A section in an Act of 1861 may be useful. This makes it an offence "unlawfully and maliciously to cause any poison or other destructive or noxious thing" to be taken by someone with the intent "to injure, aggrieve or annoy". An injured, aggrieved, or annoyed non-smoker could use reasonable force and should probably ask the smoker to stop or leave before taking the law into his or her own hands. But as the risks of passive smoking become more widely accepted, direct action and its legal aftermath will become more common.

The Government has kept curiously quiet on the legal front. All the action so far has been played out on the private stage. The Health and Safety Executive is about to publish guidelines on smoking practices at work, but resolute action is not contemplated.

Source: The Guardian 20/7/88

ASSIGNMENT ⑦

Read the following articles.

In your groups write a list of the reasons given in these extracts for why children still take up smoking, despite the risks of cancer.

Discuss the reasons. Do you agree with them? Can you think of any more reasons why children take up smoking? If so add them to the list.

Bribe them with a new car or threaten them with cancer

Or you could try setting a good example to stop your girl smoking

PARENTS try all sorts of ploys to stop their teenage daughters smoking. They resort to bribes and even threats to tackle the fastest growing band of smokers in this country.

TV health guru Miriam Stoppard agrees with the carrot-on-a-stick approach. She has promised her four children a car each if they say "no" to fags, drink and drugs.

Other worried mums and dads try shock treatment. They warn of grim consequences and point to messages like a Health Education Authority advert which shows how smoking can cause the loss of a leg.

That's Life presenter Esther Ranzten makes it clear to her children the part cigarettes played when husband Desmond Wilcox fell seriously ill.

Regular parental preaching is not always the answer of course. Junior health minister Edwina Currie lectures the entire country about the dangers of smoking, but her daughter Debbie, 13, was still having a sly whiff in the school dorm.

More than 12 per cent of 11 to 16 year girls are already hooked on the weed. And twice as many girls or boys in this age group smoke at least 50 cigarettes a week.

"Teenage girls smoke to keep up with their friends because they see it as the grown-up thing to do," says a spokeswoman for the anti-smoking group ASH. Even though cigarette advertising has been banned from magazines aimed at young women, the image of smoking as glamorous is still strong among such an impressionable age group.

So it is hardly surprising parents are using every means at their disposal to turn their kids away from cigarettes. But perhaps the best step a parent can take is to set a good example.

Surveys have shown that the children of smokers are more likely to take up the habit. In the case of Debbie Currie, it is an inescapable fact that her father Ray was a 40-a-day man until earlier this year when he saw the light.

But even if parents smoke there is evidence that their offspring will take notice if they make it clear that they disapprove. "Be firm," ASH advises. "Say that even though you smoke you made a mistake."

Surgery

Childcare expert Penelope Leach, mother of Melissa, 20, and Matthew, 23, suggests parents who smoke should insist "Please do as we say and not as we do." Possibly the most extravagant incentive is the car bonus offered by Miriam Stoppard. Her stepson Oliver, 22, has already claimed his reward - a Toyota.

Esther Rantzen's husband Desmond Wilcox underwent bypass surgery two years ago, triggered in part by his heavy smoking. Since then she has been so anti-smoking she has been known to snatch cigarettes from children's mouths in the street.

"We have made our three children very aware that smoking contributed to their father's illness" she says. The problem of girl smokers has dismayed health educationalists and many have been quick to support Mrs Currie's stand. Dr Anne Charlton said: "She is doing a marvelous job. Although I don't know why Debbie was smoking, I would sympathise with both her and her daughter."

Softly, softly mum's bedroom rule works

YOUTH worker Jackie Hubert could not believe it when she discovered her daughter, Kern, 18, was secretly smoking in their garden.

Jackie, who tries to drive home the anti-smoking message at youth clubs near her home in Brighton, said: "By the time I found out she was already on 20 a day.

"I was shocked. I've always been violently against it, and the children know it. I've heard parents say their children squander their lunch money on cigarettes. I've never given mine that temptation. They have packed lunches."

Both Jackie's parents smoke and she made sure that her children, Charlotte, five, Matthew, nine, Daniel, eleven, and Kern, were aware their grandad's chest problem was a result of smoking.

Unfair

She said: "I used my parents as an example of the dangers of smoking. And I would tell them how unpleasant it smelled." Jackie believes Kern started smoking because she was influenced by a boyfriend. But she believes a heavy-handed approach would be counter-productive.

Jackie said: "It's her decision. We've discussed it and agreed that she can only smoke in her bedroom, unless there are other smokers in the house, when that would be a bit unfair."

The softly-softly approach seems to have paid off. Kern has reduced her intake to five cigarettes a day.

Source: Today 30/9/88

Act for children

The Protection of Children (Tobacco) Bill came into force on 8 October. It is now illegal to sell any form of tobacco to children under the age of 16. The Bill was designed to remove a loophole in the 1933 Children and Young Persons' Act which permitted the sale of tobacco to children if the retailer believed the tobacco was for an adult. Since the new Bill includes all tobacco the sale to children of the new smokeless product, Skoal Bandits, is also forbidden.

BARRY FANTONI

"Beats me why I came last, sir. I only smoke TV sponsorship brands"

Source: The Times

Advertising agreement failing to protect children

One of the main aims of the voluntary agreement between the British government and the tobacco industry on tobacco promotion is to ensure that children and young people are protected and that no advertising is directed to appeal to children.

In spite of this a new report published in *Health Education*

Research found that several advertising hoardings and 60 per cent of nearby shops had tobacco advertisements which breached the rules or spirit of the voluntary agreement. The report, by Dr Amanda Amos, was based on a recent survey of tobacco promotions near places used predominantly by young people in Edinburgh.

While 93 per cent of the shops

displayed tobacco advertisements only 35 per cent had a sign visible from the outside about the law on sales of tobacco to children under 16. From the evidence of the survey findings the report concludes that the voluntary agreement is failing to promote the government's intention to protect children and young people from certain types of tobacco promotions.

Source: Ash

ASSIGNMENT 8

Look at *Nine reasons the Weed Wins*. Which categories does Dr Anne Charlton say young smokers fall into? Choose one of the categories of smoker and write the leaflet she might have written to dissuade people in this category from smoking.

ASSIGNMENT 9

Write three or four letters for an **Agony Aunt** page. These could be titled. 'How can I stop Johnny smoking? 'Why can't I smoke when my mum and dad do? and so on. Try to write the answers that might have been written.

- Think not only about the damage caused by smoking but also about why people smoke and whether their needs can be met in any other way.

NINE REASONS THE WEED WINS

ANTI-SMOKING expert Dr Anne Charlton's research group has prepared nine leaflets with advice for children battling to kick the habit.

Each Stop Smoking guide is aimed at a particular type of smoker.

- **The Sensation Smoker.** These are usually artistic and possibly shy. They like the feel of cigarettes, cigarette packs or lighters.
- **The Concentration Smoker.** They light up while working, or concentrating on a task.

- **The Pleasure Time Smoker.** Enjoys cigarettes during coffee breaks or when out in the evening.
- **The Keep Going Smoker.** Smokes out of boredom, or a general lack of interest. Many keep going smokers are unemployed.
- **The Confidence Smoker.** They believe smoking gives them the confidence to fill a role they don't feel easy in — for example, a woman in a man's world.
- **The Addicted Smoker.** This is a category rare among children.

- **The Social Confidence Smoker.** These are youngsters who use smoking to boost confidence when out socially and in company. Very common among teenage girls.
- **The Comfort Smoker.** Smokes when unhappy or during a crisis. Among girls the reasons for this kind of smoking might include exam blues, or splitting up with a boyfriend.
- **The Automatic Smoker.** Lights up cigarette after cigarette without thinking. Rare among teenagers.

Source: Today

A Representative Survey

A REPRESENTATIVE survey of 880 children in first, third and fifth years was carried out in five secondary schools in one education authority using an anonymous questionnaire. It was found that children were most aware of the cigarette brands which are most frequently associated with sponsored sporting events on TV. Children's TV viewing of a recent snooker championship sponsored by one cigarette manufacturer was positively correlated with the proportion of children associating that brand, and other brands used in TV sponsorship, with sport.

Following a snooker championship sponsored by another cigarette manufacturer, a second survey was carried out on a new sample showing that awareness of this brand and the proportion of children associating it with sport had increased from the first survey. This demonstrates that the TV sports sponsorship by tobacco manufacturers acts as cigarette advertising to children and therefore circumvents the law banning cigarette advertisements on TV.

Source: Health Education Journal

STOPPING SMOKING REDUCES

ASSIGNMENT ⑩

Look at *A representative survey* and *Carry on with the Sport*.

Both are based on questionnaires.

Decide what exactly the results of each one might tell you.
To do this you will have to consider:
1 What each one tried to find out.
2 Who the questionnaires surveyed. Were they the people with the most information?
3 What exactly were their results? Can you say in figures what each one found?

Now decide which you are most impressed by or whether neither impress you.

ASSIGNMENT ⑪

Look at the letter *Know alls*.

Write similar letters to the editor from the opposite point of view either:

1 As a parent who has just caught their child smoking the brand of cigarette which sponsors the child's favourite sport. No-one else in your household smokes.

2 As someone who has a close friend or relative, who has been a life-long smoker and who is dying of lung cancer.

CARRY ON WITH THE SPORT
The majority say yes

Killjoy campaigns for a ban on tobacco sponsorship of sport - led by the British Medical Association, the Health Education Council, ASH, the National Society for Non-Smokers, the Sports Minister, Dick Tracy and the Labour Party - do not command the support of the majority of British People.

A poll conducted for The Times by MORI, suggests that legislation to ban sports sponsorship would be unpopular and undemocratic.

An overall majority, 52% thought tobacco firms should be allowed to continue sponsoring sporting events while support for a ban was confirmed to only one in three.

Previous polls in 1983, commissioned by the Tobacco Advisory Council showed only 38% were opposed to a ban with 34% in favour.

The latest MORI figures show a clear majority opposed to the anti-smoking lobby's demands.

Interestingly, the MORI poll also challenges the main arguments of the pro-ban lobby - that children are influenced to smoke as a result of sponsored sporting events appearing on television.

Only 19% believed tobacco sponsorship of sport influenced children to smoke "a great deal". A further 21% thought children were influenced a "fair amount". But the majority thought such influence existed "hardly at all" (30%) or "not at all" (27%)

The MORI poll findings are unwelcome news to the sports Minister: Dick Tracy, who, having raised the expectations of the anti-smoking lobby with his campaign of moral favour against tobacco has now been told by the Government's business mangers of the difficulties of legislating on the eve of a general election.

His boss, Environmental Secretary Nicholas Ridley, is content to allow to continue the tobacco companies voluntary agreement under which sponsorship is controlled.

Cabinet ministers are worried about the way pressure groups are trying to cucumvent the democratic process. They understand that a sponsorship ban would be unwise when there is no overwhelming opposition to it in the country.

That view is buttressed by a Commons Motion signed by 21 backbench MPs saying "If sporting organisations want to accept sponsorship from Britain free enterprise tobacco companies, that is matter for them to decide and not for the Government.

There is currently a proposal to ban tobacco firms from sponsoring sporting events shown on TV.

Do you think the Government should:

Ban tobacco firms from sponsoring sporting events ? 33
Ban tobacco firms from sponsoring sporting events shown on TV ? 11
Allow tobacco firms to continue sponsoring sporting events ? 52
Don't know/No opinion 5

How much do you think children are influenced to smoke by the tobacco firms sponsoring sporting events which children see on television?

A great deal 19
A fair amount 21
Hardly at all 30
Not at all 27
Don't know 3

Know alls

SIR,- Having read with interest the recent arguments between ASH and FOREST in your letters column, it seems to me that the whole argument is based on the fact that people can't mind their own business!

The argument is just not based on the fact that some people should they have their way, would ban anything that they anmd other minorities do not happen to approve of.

If organisations like ASH were banned, what would be next? The anti-alcohol campaign would start putting themselves about.

Then what if alcohol were banned? Homosexuality? Videos? The list could be endless! I have noticed that over recent years - self appointed watch dogs have been on the increase, especially in certain London councils.

We already have a Health Minister, who only a few years ago was an obscure Birmingham city councillor, and is now a "health expert" seemingly knowing more about health than the BMA and the Royal College of Surgeons.

She is a self appointed "expert" on our eating habits, who beleives she is right and millions are wrong.

Finally, I respect the rights of those who don't smoke and don't smoke in confined spaces with non-smokers.

I was passing a parked car recently and noticed numerous "no-smoking" stickers in it A couple of minutes later, the driver started the engine and the car emitted a huge cloud of toxic blue smoke, which engulfed passers-by. I don't recall his apologising to them!

INFORMATION WAS OBTAINED FROM:

ASH. (Action on Smoking and Health), 5-11 Mortimer Street, London W1N 7RH.

GASP. (Group against Smoking in Public), Box 20, 37 Stokes Croft, Bristol BS1 3PY.

Health Education Authority. 78 New Oxford Street, London WC1A IAH.

FOREST. Bondway House, 3-9 Bondway, London SW18 1SJ.

CHAPTER 3

the nuclear arms debate

ASSIGNMENT ❶

Read the following poem and the article on the opposite page.

Read the poem again and then discuss what you think it is about. Here are some statements or questions to help you find your way through the poem.

1 Look at the title. Why is the poem called *Icarus Allsorts*? Find out who Icarus was. Does this help you?

2 Why are the first words in the poem written in a different type?

3 What caused the General to press the button that started the war?

4 How did the General feel about this? Give reasons. Is this a strange reaction?

5 What does the last line of the second verse refer to?

6 Look at the verse beginning 'Philip was in the countinghouse'. It is a parody of a well-known rhyme. Which one? What do you think 'parody' means?

7 How do you think the poet feels about nuclear bombs?

8 How do you feel about the poem?

ICARUS ALLSORTS

'A meteorite is reported to have landed in New England. No damage is said...'

A little bit of heaven fell
From out of the sky one day
It landed in the ocean
Not so very far away
The general at the radar screen
Rubbed his hands with glee
And grinning pressed the button
That started World War Three.

From every corner of the earth
Bombs began to fly
There were even missile jams
No traffic lights in the sky
In the times it takes to blow your nose
The people fell, the mushrooms rose

'House!' cried the fatlady
As the bingohall moved to various parts
of the town

'Raus!' cried the German butcher
as his shop came tumbling down

Philip was in the countinghouse
Counting out his money
The queen was in the parlour
Eating bread and honey

When through the window
Flew a bomb
And made them go all funny

In the time it takes to draw a breath
Or eat a toadstool, instant death

The rich
Huddled outside the doors of their fallo
shelters
Like drunken carolsingers

The poor
Clutching shattered televisions
And last week's editions of T.V. Times
(but the very last)

Civil defence volunteers
With their tin hats in one hand
And their heads in the other

CND supporters
Their ban the bomb badges beginning t
rust
Have scrawled 'I told you so' in the du

A little bit of heaven fell
From out of the sky one day
It landed in Vermont
North-Eastern U.S.A.
The general at the radar screen
He should have got the sack
But that wouldn't bring
Three thousand million, seven hundred
and sixty eight
people back,

Would it?

ROGER McGOUG

Are You For Or Against Nuclear Weapons?

Nobody wants a nuclear war, but there are opposing views as to how it can be prevented. The **Campaign for Nuclear Disarmament** (CND) believes Britain should renounce nuclear weapons first as an example to other countries (unilateral disarmament). **Peace Through Nato** (PTN) wants multilateral disarmament in which everyone gets rid of their weapons through negotiations.

NATO   **CND**

PEACE THROUGH NATO

Martin Smith, a 24 year old Yorkshireman, works for Peace Through NATO. His job involves speaking at meetings and in schools, recruiting new supporters, organising information stands at shows and exhibitions throughout the country and answering general queries. He first became aware of NATO at University and joined his local student group in 1983.

NATO has been saying for over 20 years that we want Multilateral disarmament which means that more than one country would be involved in removing and destroying weapons. Groups like CND says that this sounds fine but doesn't actually work because the arms talks get nowhere, but in 1987 America and Russia signed a treaty to get rid of an entire class of nuclear weapons and further agreements to remove more nuclear (and non-nuclear) weapons are expected soon.

Today, most people would agree that President Gorbachev is making some real and positive changes in Russia, but he is also meeting a great deal of opposition both from people who think he is going too far and those who believe he is doing enough. It is quite possible that he could be overthrown or simply lose heart given the problems he faces and that the reforms could fizzle out. In Eastern Europe there is a lot of uncertainty at the moment and no-one really knows what the final outcome of the current upheavals will be.

It is therefore still too early to be thinking about doing away with NATO or with ALL the West's nuclear weapons. Mr. Gorbachev himself said at the Malta Summit meeting with President Bush in 1989 that he isn't demanding the end of NATO or the Warsaw Pact - NATO's equivalent in the East. The West should not be hasty in doing away completely with the sytem of nuclear deterrence which has served it so well for 40 years.

NATO has repeatedly made clear that "none of our weapons will ever be used except in response to an attack". Whilst the threat of attack can never be COMPLETELY eliminated, the 1990's should - we hope - see a continued reduction in tension and the numbers of weapons in Europe both East and West.

CND

Phil Woodford, aged 21, is a student at the London School of Economics. He joined CND in 1982, and still sees the issue of nuclear disarmament as being one of the most important facing the world. He has been a member of CND's National Executive Committee.

Supporters of nuclear weapons should be made to answer one simple question: Why do WE need them, when most countries in the world do without them? Few people argue that Iran, Iraq and South Africa should have their nuclear stockpiles in order to defend themselves. What makes Britain so special?

Since the Second World War, it has always been argued that the Soviet Union represented a huge threat to the West. Nuclear weapons and the western alliance, NATO, were needed to defend us from attack. In the 1990s, such an idea seems very outdated. More and more people, of all political persuasions, are starting to question the huge sums of money we spend on weapons. Whilst two-thirds of the world is threatened with starvation, the other third devises expensive means of destroying the planet. Any alien observing us from outer space would clearly think that we were mad! Our current defence policy is similar to someone setting up a burglar alarm, which blows up their house as soon as an intruder enters. Maybe burglars would be deterred by such an alarm. But would any sensible householder gamble with such a dangerous strategy? They only need to be wrong once for their house to be completely destroyed. Likewise, those people who argue for nuclear "deterrence" only need to be wrong once for our planet to be destroyed. A policy of suicide rather than defence.

CND is a movement which is open to everyone, because it doesn't matter whether you're a stockbroker, a steelworker or a school student - nuclear weapons threaten the lives of people everywhere. We look forward to the day when the army must hold jumbles sales to pay for its weapons, and when governments spend their money on feeding the starving. It's now time for everyone to think about where their priorities lie.

ASSIGNMENT ②

Could a mistake of the kind described in the poem *Icarus Allsorts* be made? The article on page 35 will help you to think about the answer to this.

Take a vote at this point to see how many of the group are in favour of nuclear weapons. Note the figure.

ASSIGNMENT ③

Put a heading **Peace through NATO** and another **CND** (Campaign for Nuclear Disarmament). Make a list of the arguments both make to substantiate their point of view.

ASSIGNMENT ④

Readers of the **Peace Through Nato** and **CND** articles on page 35 were asked to reply in a letter stating their feelings about the arguments given. Write the letter explaining how you feel about the articles. Explain whether or not you are in favour of nuclear weapons giving reasons for your views.

ASSIGNMENT ⑤

Read the following material: *Nato's armies lag behind Eastern bloc, Mayor of Hiroshima's Speech* and *Hiroshima and Nagasaki*.
(**Note:** Hikabusha was the name given to those directly affected by the dropping of the bombs on the two cities.)

What is *Nato's armies lag behind Eastern bloc* diagram saying?

How would **Peace through Nato** say that this supported their argument?

What does the mayor of Hiroshima argue about nuclear weapons?

Why does he call the bomb dropped on Hiroshima 'a single toy-like weapon'? The **CND** article on page 35 should help you answer this.

If the Russians invade using conventional weapons should the West use nuclear arms against them? Write about a page arguing for or against such use.

Nato's armies lag behind East bloc

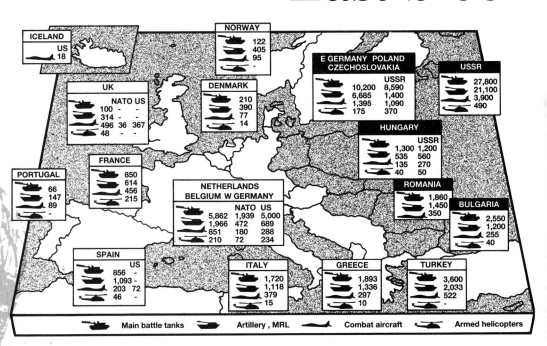

Source: The Times 19/10/88

ASSIGNMENT ⑥

Imagine you are a member of **Youth CND** or a Youth Branch of **Peace through NATO.** A competition has been launched that invites young people to promote the organisation. You must state in as convincing a way as possible reasons for the organisation's adopted viewpoint. The winning entry will be mass produced for nationwide distribution.

- Remember to use the logo of the organisation.
- Summon as many facts as possible to substantiate your point of view.
- Think about the way you will write this.
- Is a question/answer format a useful one to adopt?
- Illustrations will help you to make the leaflet eye-catching – these could be copied if you are not a good artist.
- Remember to use persuasive language to try and convince the reader that they should adopt your view.

MAYOR OF HIROSHIMA'S SPEECH

My name is Takeshi Araki - Mayor of the City of Hiroshima and President of the World Conference of Mayors for Peace through Inter-city Solidarity.

In August 1945 mankind made a terrible mistake - the dropping of atomic bombs on the two cities of Hiroshima and Nagasaki. However, I have not come before you to rail against the dropping of these atomic bombs.

Rather, I come before you in the spirit of the epitaph carved on the Memorial Cenotaph in Hiroshima: "Let all the souls here rest in peace; for we shall not repeat the evil." This epitaph is at once a prayer for the repose of the bomb's victims' souls and a powerful pledge on behalf of all mankind, past, present and future. It is, in short, the spirit of Hiroshima. Hiroshima has undergone great tragedy, but it has also transcended the hatreds and overcome countless difficulties to be reborn as a City of International Peace and Culture. With a population of over 1 million, Hiroshima has dedicated itself to working for the abolition of all nuclear weapons and the establishment of true world peace.

Nuclear weapons were still in their infancy when those early prototypes were dropped on Hiroshima and Nagasaki, but the devastation was total. The single toy-like weapon snuffed out the lives of 140,000 people and laid waste to our city. In Hiroshima myself that fateful day, I can never forget the gruesome scenes that awaited me everywhere I turned. Those victims who were not killed outright suffer the after effects even today. Aside from the direct Hibakusha, there are about 360,000 people living lives of torture, their health destroyed by secondary radiation and other bomb-related causes. It is this message that I would like to impress upon the world's politicians as eloquently and as vividly as I possibly can.

For if they will recognise this truth, they may also come to realise what barbarity the development and possession of nuclear weapons is and what an unpardonable evil it is.

Hiroshima is more than a witness to history. It is also a powerful warning about the future of our world.

STATEMENT BY MAYOR OF HIROSHIMA AT THE 3RD SPECIAL SESSION OF THE UNITED NATIONS GENERAL ASSEMBLY FOR DISARMAMENT JUNE 9TH 1988.

How many people were killed?

Because of the utter devastation caused by the bombs, the immediate death toll was difficult to calculate. Japanese figures estimate that in the first four months, between 130,000 and 140,000 died in Hiroshima, and 60,000 to 70,000 in Nagasaki. The eventual total is probably nearer 200,000 in Hiroshima and 100,000 in Nagasaki.

What kind of bombs were they?

They were both atomic bombs. The bomb that was dropped on Hiroshima had a core of Uranium 235 and a destructive yield of about 12.5 kilotons or 20,000 tons of TNT.

The Nagasaki bomb was known as 'Fat Man' because of 'its cheerful rotundity and consequent association with Churchill!' It had a plutonium core and a destructive yield of 22.2 kilotons. By comparison a cruise missile has a destructive power of 200 kilotons.

Source: CND

ASSIGNMENT ⑦

Read the article *Non-Threatening Deterrent Is the Basis for Peace.*

Note: *Multilateral disarmament means all countries getting rid of nuclear weapons at the same time. Unilateral refers to one nation on its own taking this initiative.*

Now discuss and answer the following questions:

1 What is a deterrent?

2 What does the writer mean by a non-threatening deterrent?

3 What does the phrase 'Better Red than Dead' mean?

4 What does 'Soviet expansionism' mean?

5 Are you afraid the Russians will invade Britain? Give reasons for your answer.

6 Is this 'Russian threat' why we have nuclea weapons in Britain?

7 The writer states that even if we gave up ou weapons we would still be in danger. Why i this?

8 The writer suggests that nuclear weapons kee the peace. How can you prove or disprove thi view? Think of examples in world events to hel you.

9 According to the writer how would the Kremli view unilateral disarmament? Do you agree?

10 How do you as an individual and as a group fee about this issue? Should Britain disarm unilater ally – on her own; or should we wait for *a* nations to do so?

Take a vote on the issue as a group.

NON-THREATENING DETERRENT IS THE BASIS FOR PEACE

maintains Alan Lee Williams

One of the arguments for unilateral disarmament is that it is better to be alive in a Soviet dominated world than to be blown up in a nuclear holocaust. In other words: 'Better Red Than Dead.' It is maintained that it is better to give up nuclear weapons and face the possibility of being taken over by the Soviet Union than to face nuclear war.

Unfortunately, however, the choice between accepting Soviet expansionism and nuclear war does not necessarily exist. The fact that a medium nuclear power no longer possesses nuclear weapons will not eliminate the possibility of a breakout of nuclear war. A nuclear war may still occur between the United States and the Soviet Union, in which case a country such as Britain would suffer great damage for nuclear fall-out and radiation alone.

In this argument, I see again the lack of understanding in the minds of the unilateralist groups and some peace movements as to the importance of nuclear weapons as enforcers of international peace and stability. It is crucial for these groups to come to grips with the fact that

weapons do not cause wars, they are merely the symptoms of conflict. Were a medium nuclear power unilaterally to disarm, the Kremlin would most likely interpret it as a sign of weakness, and the defenceless country would no doubt be subject to Soviet pressure in a crisis situation.

Supporters of CND claim that this would be a better alternative to nuclear war. What they fail to understand is that it is not an 'either/or' situation. This would not decrease the chances of war. Since the knowledge of how to build

nuclear weapons will always exist, the way to guarantee peace is not through giving up weapons but through learning how to procure and store arms in such a way as to provide a credible but not threatening deterrent force. It is this belief that has guided me on defence matters during my years as a Labour Member of Parliament and, more recently, as an individual member of the Social Democratic Party. If Britain is to remain a nuclear power, and I believe it should, then it must have the best nuclear deterrent available.

Help Keep The NATO Flags Flying

ASSIGNMENT 8

Study *Deadly Myths, If You Fold A Thousand Paper Cranes... and Which Way to Nuclear Disarmament?* Write the speech you would deliver in a debate on whether **NATO** should disarm unilaterally or not.

- Look back at all the material about nuclear disarmament you have read so far.
- Are you in favour of or opposed to nuclear weapons?
- What are your reasons? Could you include some of these in your speech?

DEADLY MYTHS

'THE BOMB HAS KEPT THE PEACE IN EUROPE FOR 40 YEARS

That's just a guess. Nobody knows what would have happened if nuclear weapons hadn't been invented. But one thing is certain. No arms race has ever prevented war - only made it more terrible when it came.

Today the build-up of nuclear weapons on both sides in Europe makes war more likely, not less. It also stops us finding peaceful solutions to the problems of our divided continent.

Outside Europe there have been dozens of wars since 1945 killing millions of people. The Bomb hasn't stopped these wars, even though many involved countries with their own nuclear weapons.

'ONLY THE BOMB STOPS THE RUSSIANS FROM INVADING WESTERN EUROPE

You don't have to believe the Russians are pacifists to disagree with this. What would the Russians gain by taking over Western Europe? They already have problems in Eastern Europe, without taking on ours as well. But even if they wanted, they couldn't. There is no Soviet superiority, either of nuclear weapons or conventional forces. Experts agree that 'the conventional overall balance is still such as to make general military aggression a highly risky undertaking for either side'.(*The Military Balance, 1985-6, Institute of Strategic Studies, London.*)

Source: CND

IF YOU FOLD A THOUSAND PAPER CRANES ...

The children's monument was erected in 1958 after the death of Sakado Sasaki. She was two when the bomb exploded, and seemed to be a normal healthy girl, but she developed leukaemia from delayed radiation effects.
Sakado has been called the Anne Frank of Hiroshima and she symbolises the thousands of young people who suffered from the bomb.

According to the legend, Sakado was very brave in hospital. She wrote in her diary that she didn't want to die, but she managed to stay cheerful when her classmates came to visit her. She folded paper cranes. There is an old belief in Japan that a crane can live a thousand years, and to fold a thousand paper cranes will protect you from illness. When she died Sakado had only folded 964. Her friends finished her missing cranes and put them all in her coffin. The young people of Hiroshima, unable to bear watching their friends dying, erected a monument to Sakado in the Peace Park to remind the world what the bomb had done to the children who experienced it. At the base of the monument hung with strings of coloured paper cranes are the words:

This is our cry, this is our prayer : peace in the world.

Source: CND

CHRISTIAN CND
St Luke 6:27,28 **PLOUGHSHARE JULY 1987**

WHICH WAY
TO NUCLEAR DISARMAMENT?
INF AGREEMENT SIGNED DECEMBER '87

THE WRONG WAY

THE RIGHT WAY

MEDIUM RANGE MISSILES TO GO —
CND GOT IT WRONG!

PEACE THROUGH NATO

Published by Peace Through NATO, 46-47 Chancery Lane, London WC2A 1JB. Printed by C.C.O., 16 Stadium Way, Reading RG3 6BX

ASSIGNMENT 9

Ask your science teacher for any information they might have about the effects of radiation.
Read the extract from *When the Wind Blows* by Raymond Briggs (pages 42 and 43).

1 What caused the woman's sickness?

2 Were they wise to go outside? Why?

3 What effect did the bomb have on the garden?

4 What do you think of the comments 'They didn't blow up the sun, thank goodness.' 'Oh, no dear, science is still in its infancy'?

5 What does this tell you about the couple's knowledge of the bomb and its effects?

6 Do you think many people are like them?

7 What do you know about 'Fall Out'?

8 What is likely to happen to the weather after a nuclear attack?

9 'What could be purer than water.' Is this statement true?

10 Do you think we are better equipped to deal with a nuclear attack than the Japanese were?

11 Are there antidotes to combat radiation sickness?

12 Why was the book called *When the Wind Blows*?

13 What point do you think the cartoonist was making?

ASSIGNMENT 10

There is to be a referendum to decide whether or not we as a nation should have nuclear weapons. Design a pamphlet explaining your views on this issue and persuading people to adopt your viewpoint.

There is to be a live radio debate between the public, members of **Peace through NATO** and **CND**. The discussion follows a Commons statement in which a woman MP said:

I think it is immoral to spend the people's money on bombs that are never used, not that I think we should use them God Forbid! I just wonder at the wasted money! In a short space of time they are outdated, so we replace them. Why? Because we believe scare-mongers who suggest that without them we will be invaded by the Russians. As if they would want to! We waste billions each year on nuclear arms and weaponry.

Let's feed the poor, keep our old people warm and secure, buy books for our schools and stop hospitals from crumbling around our ears - and the National Health Service with it. I say we have better things to spend our money on than nuclear arms!

Script the discussion that might follow such a controversial statement.

- Write it in play form.
- Make up names for the people concerned.
- Think carefully about what the MP suggested.
- Is it as easy as that?

INFORMATION WAS OBTAINED FROM:

- The Ministry of Defence.
- The British Atlantic Committee. 5 St James Place, London SW1A 1NP.
- Peace through NATO. 46-47 Chancery Lane, London WC2.
- CND. 22-24 Underwood Street, London N1 7JG.
- Hiroshima Memorial Hall. 1-2 Nakajima-Cho, Naka-Ku, Hiroshima City, 730 JAPAN.

THE FOLLOWING MORNING

Better try and eat something today, dear

I was sick three times in the night and my headache is even worse

Let's have a walk round the garden, dear. I've just read it's only 48 hours in the Inner Core or Refuge; not 14 days. A bit of fresh air is all we need. I'll get a nice lettuce

Crumbs! Look at the door! The paint is all gone - scorched down to the wood

Never mind, dear. You said you'd burn it off one day

The leaves have all gone off the apple tree, ducks

Oh yes. What a shame

Still, it will be lovely in the Spring

It is Spring, dear

The heat has affected the hedge, love

The beans look a bit shrivelled

And I think the lettuces have evaporated

They do have a high water content

Can you see any Fall Out falling out, James?

No, the sun is shining

They didn't blow up the sun, thank goodness

Oh no, dear. Science is still in its Infancy

What does the Fall Out look like, dear?

I don't know. The Governmental Directive neglects to mention how the populace could recognise it. I expect it's a bit like snow, ducks

The grass looks a funny colour

Yes, I'll pop down to Mr. Spong's tomorrow and get some Bone Meal and Dried Blood

He may be closed due to The Bomb, dear

What? Old Spong? Miss a day's trade? Not him. He'd rather die

It's a really lovely day. Perhaps The Bomb has brought some nice weather. We could do with some sun

It needs something to bring the garden on

The milkman's not been yet. He's late

Oh well, that's logical. He's bound to be a bit late after The Bomb

Perhaps he's been Called Up - to fight, or something.

Oh yes, well.....maybe, but they'd have got a woman or something

Very quiet isn't it?

Yes, funny. No trains

No traffic

I expect they're all having a good lie-in after The Bomb

Terrible smell of burning.....

Oh yes, well.... bound to be - that's logical

It's like roast meat

Yes. Roast dinners. I expect people are having their Sunday dinners early this week - due to the unexpected circumstances

The road's gone all funny. Seems to have melted a bit

I expect that's why the milkman's late. He's got stuck somewhere

I wonder if there's a proper War on? I wonder who's winning?

Never mind. It'll all be in the papers, dear

Come to think of it – he's late, too

He missed us altogether yesterday

Well, you can't expect things to be normal after The Bomb. Difficulties will be experienced throughout the Duration of the Emergency Period

Normality will only be assumed after the Censation of Hostilities

Oh dear – I think I'm going to be sick again

There, there, ducks, all better now

I had the most terrible diarrhoea this morning

Nerves, dear. Just nerves. I'm the same and I'm a man

Let's sit in the sun for a bit

Don't you think we ought to clear up, dear?

Yes, later on. I feel a bit weak and dizzy. We'll make a start soon

Oooh! Suppose Jerry comes this afternoon!

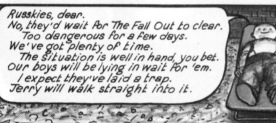

Russkies, dear.
No, they'd wait for The Fall Out to clear. Too dangerous for a few days. We've got plenty of time. The situation is well in hand, you bet. Our boys will be lying in wait for 'em. I expect they've laid a trap. Jerry will walk straight into it.

Hullo....
sun's gone in.
Cloud coming up.
Looks like rain....

LATER

It's raining. I'm going in

RAIN! Yes! We can save it!

Don't you get wet, James! You'll catch your death

We'll be all right for water for a while now, dear

Do you think rain water is all right to drink?

Oh yes! 'Course it is! There's nothing purer than rainwater 'is there? Everybody knows that

Perhaps I'd better boil it. Best to be on the safe side

Oh yes, I suppose so. We don't want to take any unnecessary risks

It may prejudice our chance of survival

What do you mean, James? We have survived, haven't we?

Yes, I know, but after The Bombs on Japan, people died ages later .... I forget exactly why....

Perhaps they didn't take precautions

Yes. I expect they neglected to do the correct thing.
And anyway that was years ago. Science was in its infancy.
We're better equipped to deal with the situation in the light of modern scientific knowledge

Yes, nowadays there's bound to be all sorts of anti-totes and protectives

When the Medics get through, they'll probably just spray us with some anti-tote, give us a couple of pills and in no time we'll be as right as rain

Source: When the Wind Blows by Raymond Briggs

CHAPTER 4

the loch ness monster

There have been repeated sightings of a 'monster' in Loch Ness from the year 565 AD, when Saint Colomba sighted something unusual that could have been a monster. In 1933 the loch was opened to tourism in a big way with the completion of the A82 motor road along the north shore. Sightings of a beast in the loch increased in frequency from that time on and began with the sighting reported on page 45. One explanation for this sudden rush of sightings was that during the blasting that occurred when the new road was being built a series of Jules Verne-like caverns were opened up, releasing creatures into the loch. Whether that is possible and whether there are monsters in the loch is for you to decide!

 ASSIGNMENT ❶

Read the article *Strange Spectacle on Loch Ness*.

Classic photo of Nessie shot in April of 1934 by Lt.-Col. Robert K. Wilson, M.D.

STRANGE SPECTACLE ON LOCH NESS

What was it?
(from a Correspondent)

Loch Ness has for generations been credited with being the home of a fearsome-looking monster, but, somehow or other, the "water-kelpie," as this legendary creature is called, has always been regarded as a myth, if not a joke. Now, however, comes the news that the beast has been seen once more, for on Friday of last week, a well-known business man, who lives near Inverness, and his wife (a University graduate), when motoring along the north shore of the loch, not far from Abriachan Pier, were startled to see a tremendous upheaval on the loch, which, previously had been as calm as the proverbial mill-pond. The lady was the first to notice the disturbance, which occurred fully three quarters of a mile from the shore, and it was her sudden cries to stop that drew her husband's attention to the water.

There, the creature disported itself, rolling and plunging for fully a minute, its body resembling that of a whale, and the water cascading and churning like a simmering cauldron.
Soon, however, it disappeared in a boiling mass of foam. Both onlookers confessed that there was something uncanny about the whole thing, for they realised that here was no ordinary denizen of the depths, because, apart from its enormous size, the beast, in taking the final plunge, sent out waves that were big enough to have been caused by a passing steamer. The watchers waited for almost half an hour in the hope that the monster (if such it was) would come to the surface again; but they had seen the last of it. Questioned as to the length of the beast, the lady stated that, judging by the state of the water in the affected areas, it seemed to be many feet long.

It will be remembered that a few years ago, a party of Inverness anglers reported that when crossing the loch in a rowing boat, they encountered an unknown creature, whose bulk, movements, and the amount of water it displaced at once suggested that it was either a very large seal, a porpoise, or indeed, the monster itself!

But the story, which duly appeared in the press, received scant attention and less credence. In fact, most of those people who aired their views on the matter did so in a manner that bespoke feelings of the utmost scepticism.

It should be mentioned that, so far as is known, neither seals nor porpoises have ever been known to enter Loch Ness. Indeed, in the case of the latter, it would be utterly impossible for them to do so, and, as to the seals, it is a fact that though they have on rare occasions been seen on the River Ness, their presence in Loch Ness has never once been definitely established.

Courier 2 May 1933

ASSIGNMENT ②

Answer the following questions.

1 What other name is given in the passage for the legendary monster?

2 When and where was the monster sighted?

3 Why do you think the fact that the lady is a University graduate is mentioned?

4 Imagine that you are the man or woman who sighted the monster. Relate to a friend the details of the incident as it is told in the passage.

5 What evidence is given in the passage to suggest that this wasn't the first sighting of the monster?

6 What evidence is there to suggest that some people do not take the monster seriously?

7 The photo above the article was taken by another person a year after the reported sighting. People say that a camera never lies. With your reasons explain whether you think this photo is a real photo of the actual monster or not.

8 What logical reasons have people put forward to explain away the sightings of the monster?

9 Basing your answer on the introduction, the photo and this article, say whether you think a monster exists or not, giving your reasons.

ASSIGNMENT ③

Look at the publicity material from the *Loch Ness Exhibition Centre*.
Read the article *Nessie: Sonar and Yet So Far*.

Discuss the following questions in your groups.

1 Does the reporter believe in the Loch Ness Monster?

2 Why does he think the whole exercise was mounted here?

3 Why might it be important for Loch Ness that so many reporters from all over the world turned up?

4 Why do you think so many people from all over the world turned up for the Loch Ness Monster Search?

5 What does the reporter think of Adrian Shine?

6 Are his views of Adrian Shine important in deciding whether the Loch Ness Monster exists or if the expedition will find it?

On the A82
Relaxation, excitement, information for all the family – the ideal all-weather stop,

14 miles from Inverness	47 miles from Aviemore
174 miles from Edinburgh	52 miles from Fort William
68 miles from Skye	19 from Fort Augustus
14 miles from Beauly	24 miles from Strathpeffer
1½ miles from Castle Urquhart	

LOCH NESS CENTRE

Drumnadrochit
Inverness-shire

OFFICIAL LOCH NESS MONSTER EXHIBITION

"*. . . no further doubt in my mind that large animals exist in Loch Ness.*" (Sir Peter Scott).

See the evidence from 565 A.D. in pictures, film, audio visuals and many (new) exhibits.

See the famous "flipper" in 3D.
Board the biggest inflatable in the world and study the scenes.
See the smallest-ever manned submersible.
Look at the natural history of the waters of Loch Ness – all alive, alive-o!

THE NEW
NESSIE'S MONSTER CHEF & GRILL

Fast, good family food, and new rooftop restaurant.

Plus the Monster Hunter's Bar with panoramic views of the loch and glen.
Not forgetting the Monster Ice Cream shop, the Souvenir and Bookshop, bar facilities and outside lunch and relaxing area, toilets.

And also the snug, clean, new Loch Ness Centre Hotel – 28 rooms with private bath.

The Loch Ness Monster Exhibition
We've seen it at
DRUMNADROCHIT

LOCH NESS WOOLLENS (KILTMAKER)
(Tel: 321)

for kilts, woollens, souvenirs, and superb range of Highland products.

The Centre also has a lochan (small lake) and in it floats a "*life-size*" realistic model of "*Nessie*" (see front of this leaflet). Take unique holiday photos of the family with "Nessie" right there!
Finally, watch live glass-blowing at the "Iceberg".   And study the International House of Heraldry.
   Whether you have a few minutes or several hours – don't miss the Loch Ness Monster Exhibition.
Exhibition open 9 a.m. to 9.30 p.m. everyday. Closes earlier before July and after August. Meals available until about 9 p.m.
— Tel: Drumnadrochit (04562) 573 —

Source: Loch Ness Exhibition Centre

Nessie: Sonar and yet so far

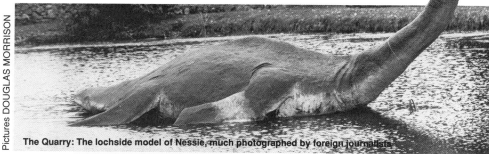

Pictures DOUGLAS MORRISON

The Quarry: The lochside model of Nessie, much photographed by foreign journalists

Michael O'Flaherty"s in-depth probe into the mysteries of Loch Ness

A WHITE sun dazzles on the withering waters. The dark waves break and froth; and, after sampling one or more of the 10 malt whiskies available in the Clansman hotel, people swear they have seen the legendary monster.

Everything here is monster. There are monster burgers, monster sandwiches, monster bars, monster chocolate.

And of course there is the Loch Ness Monster. Or is there?

Come in Boat 16. Your time is up. The searching sonar probing the 720ft depths of this dark brooding loch has fixed on a "moving object" 200 ft beneath the peaty waves.

Is it a fish? Is it a reptile? Is it a monster? Is it ... is it Nessie? Well, they can't quite say yet. It's big and it moves and the ITN camara crew just happen to be aboard at the time. Tomorrow, says an observer, it will be the turn of the BBC.

Tony Harmsworth, director of the Loch Ness Centre says: "We certainly don't expect to have a conclusion during this operation. We do not expect to prove or disprove whether there is a monster."

TEMPTED

So what are we all doing here, a monstrosity of media men from every continent?

"We never said we would find the monster," says Mr. Harmsworth disarmingly.

Nessiteras Rhombopteryx*, as naturalist Sir Peter Scott named the beast some years ago, has never come with guarantees but 25 TV crews and 250 news-paper men have come in hope. Tempted here by the juicy words of the PR men promoting Operation Deepscan, are swaggering Amercians in tartan caps, hyperactive Japanese in business suits, serious and frantic story-seeking men and women from France, Germany, Holland, Switzerland, Sweden, Brazil and Australia

There's even someone from the Ontario Angler and Hunter. Everyone's looking for his fishing rod.

The tourist board is looking to profits at hotels and bars

Blow the tourists! The Press is here! All seeking that ultimate in-depth interview.

For some reason, William Hill, bookmakers of that ilk, have reduced the odds of finding Nessie from 200 to 100-1.

But first the find must be verified by the Natural History Museum who fear an influx of bloodied corpses representing, perhaps, a gambler's last throw. It is chaotic. People are scrambling on and off boats and gibbering in 20 different languages.

"In Japan," says a Japanese, "the Loch Ness monster is above Mrs. Thatcher in public interest. She is taught in schools."

Which is why this TV crew upped camaras and hastened from Blackpool to Loch Ness when news of the hunt became known.

This is the biggest ever investigation of Loch Ness. It would have cost £1m but publicity-conscious companies donated sonars, ships and myriad other goodies.

Twenty of the small boats, a posh and gleaming Dunkirk, swept out from the small harbour at Drumnadrochit yesterday, sonars blipping and bleeping.

BRIDADE

Among the shipmates were young seafarers from Operation Drake, and Viscount Althorp, Di-ly reporting for NBC, and the international brigade of prospective Nessie finders.

The ships were sweeping the 23-mile-long loch from top to bottom in an operation lasting the week-end.

But sadly it is one that will have no result except perhaps to find a fews shoals of fish or chunks of the wreckage of Sir John Cobb's board which broke up when he was attempting the water speed record in 1952.

Echo, Ec ho . . . it's another sounding.

"But we won't be able to analyse it until much later, probably a year or two," said Mr. Harmsworth.

"We had a sonar expedition in 1982 and we hade 40 contacts then. All appeared to move."

So did the Pressmen ....Away. Japanese bickered. Americans yawned. Brazilians screamed. The man from the Ontario Angler and Hunter put away his fishing rod and appeared to get out his shotgun.

"A monster is in the eye of the beholder," said the supercilious Mr. Adrian Shine, 37, the expedition leader.

He's been in Loch Ness on and off for 14 years.

His real job is selling the greaseproof papers people put between hamburgers and in his other role he calls himself a naturalist.

"I work in my spare time. I'm on two month's leave of absence," explains the bright Mr. Shine, who has brought us all flocking to Loch Ness.

The sonar people are paying him £1,000.00 - sonar, so good - and lending him £20,000.00 worth of equipment.

You have to applaud his audacity. Scientific qualifications? "None," says Mr. Shine, a former grammar school boy from Wimbledon.

Worse, he doesn't even believe in the monster.

"I have the scientists. I provide the umbrella," says Mr. Shine, who tells the boat crews through a megaphone to "keep the faith."

MYTHS

So what are we doing here when he says he won't find the monster?

"That's your problem," he says, shaking his neatly combed Captain Birdseye"s beard.

"The monster is a media myth," he adds. "I certainly would not expect to drag a reptile out kicking and screaming. But you can't kill myths with science."

Someone wisely says: "They killed the Man in the Moon."

Nessie lies low. But there's a model of her in a pond by the expedition centre, and the foreign journalists rush there to take pictures.

Nessie at least knows what Sir Peter Scott meant.

*Nessiteras Rhombopteryx is an anagram which means" Monster hoax by Sir Peter S.

"Keep the faith, urged Captain Birdseye"

Source: Daily Express 10/10/87

ASSIGNMENT ④

Imagine that you are a radio reporter who is tired of waiting for the sonar expedition to find a monster. You have to record a piece on Loch Ness to be broadcast on the midday news programme but you decide to do a five-minute article on Drumnachdrochit instead. Write your script using the information in the article *Nessie: Sonar and Yet So Far* and the publicity material from the *Loch Ness Exhibition Centre*. This could of course be taped on to a cassette. Before you start this work discuss the following points carefully.

What are the hotel and surrounding area like?

Are they a tourist attraction?

Is this a good thing?

Would the area benefit if the monster were found?

What would happen if it were proved to be a hoax?

What equipment is being used to search for the monster?

How many media people are present?

What is their mood?

How would you feel if you were just waiting for the monster to appear?

Is the following information useful to know. 'In Japan the Loch Ness Monster is above Mrs Thatcher in public interest. She is taught in schools.' How could this help your radio script?

Think carefully about the structure of this work.

Does it matter if you believe or don't believe in the monster's existence?

Does the reporter believe in the monster theory?

What are your reasons for feeling this way?

Would you adopt this attitude? Why?

ASSIGNMENT ⑤

Read *Why I Believe* and *Naming the Loch Ness Monster*. Look again at the last paragraph of *Sonar and Yet . . .*.What reasons does it give for Nessie's Latin name? In *Naming the Loch Ness Monster* and *Why I Believe in the Loch Ness Monster* other reasons are given. Explain in about half a page which one you think is correct and why.

ASSIGNMENT ⑥

Look closely at Sir Peter Scott's article *Why I Believe In The Loch Ness Monster*. Explain his opening paragraph. What point is he making? He has never sighted the monster. Why does he think that a large creature or creatures might exist in Loch Ness? List the evidence he uses. Does he think or say the existence of *Nessiteras rhombopteryx* has been totally proved?

Naming the Loch Ness Monster

It is proposed that the large animal species living in Loch Ness be called *Nessiteras rhombopteryx*. Scott and Rines (nov. genus and species, the only species is automatically the type species) with the common names, the Nessie or Loch Ness monster.

The generic name *Nessiteras*, a neuter noun, is a composite word combining the name of the Loch with the Greek work *teras*, genitive *teratos*, which was used from Homer onwards to mean a marvel or wonder, and in a concrete sense for a range of monsters which aroused awe, amazement and often fear.

The specific name *rhombopteryx* is a combination of the Greek *rhombos*, a diamond or lozenge shape, and the Greek *pteryx* meaning a fin or wing. Thus the species is the Ness monster with diamond fin.

Source: Nature

WHY I BELIEVE IN THE LOCH NESS MONSTER

by Sir Peter Scott

BRITAIN'S BEST KNOWN NATURAL-IST (AND A MEMBER OF THE LOCH NESS INVESTIGATION BUREAU SINCE ITS FOUNDATION IN 1961) HAS CAREFULLY EXAMINED ALL THE EVIDENCE FOR THE EXISTENCE OF THE LOCH NESS MONSTER. HERE ARE HIS CONCLUSIONS.

True or false? "The earth is flat." "The coelacanth became extinct 70 million years ago." "Space travel is utter bilge." "The Apollo 'moon landings' were all filmed in the Hollywood studios." "No further large animal species remain to be discovered." "There can be no such thing as the Loch Ness Monster." "There is a population of large animals in Loch Ness." Which is the odd one out? For some strange reason the mystery surrounding An Niseag, the great beastie of Loch Ness, arouses enormous interest, not to say passion. The reasons for this are, like the subject, obscure.

My own interest in Nessie began some sixteen years ago when I read the book More Than a Legend by Mrs Constance Whyte. With Richard Fitter, David James and Mrs Whyte I was one of the founders of the Loch Ness Investigation Bureau. The intention of the Bureau was primarily to act as a centre for the receipt of any further evidence that might come to light on the presence of large animals in the loch, and to organise a camera watch. I spent one week and a number of shorter periods watching the loch during all daylight hours. I had the opportunity to dive with an aqualung and to fly over it for a number of hours in a glider. More recently I have again been swimming underwater in the loch, but I have never seen anything which might have been a Nessie.

When in 1960 Tim Dinsdale obtained some film which he believed to be of a monster, and when in addition striking still photographic evidence was produced, supported by three independent groups of witnesses, a meeting was called by the Bureau at the Linnean Society to which a small number of zoologists was invited. A recommendation was made that more official investigations should be undertaken - but research remained mainly the province of individual enthusiasts who were widely regarded as crackpots, although some university based sonar research was undertaken.

In spite of honest error, misidentification, wishful thinking, exaggeration, hoaxes and falsehoods, there was in my view, always a hard core of the accumulating evidence that could not be explained away in terms of known phenomena.

And then I saw Bob Rine's new photographic evidence. Two of the 1972 photographs, taken about a minute apart, show what seems to be a flipper or paddle of diamond shape and a part of the adjacent rough skinned body. In one there are shadowy indications of what might be an underlying rib structure. There is sufficient minor difference in the shape of the flipper, its orientation in the frame, and its attachment to the body, in the two photographs to rule out the possibility that the object is stationery or a solid model. These differences are strongly suggestive of the swimming limb of an animal and the implications are that it is a right hind limb.

To me the existence of the second flipper photograph more than doubles the significance of the first. The possibility that the large sonar echoes could have been submersible equipment being used by hoaxers to place artifacts in front of the camera was carefully considered and rejected as unrealistic.

The flipper photographs are probably the most significant to zoologists, but two of the 1975 photographs seem especially striking to the non-zoologist. The first of these - the head or 'Gargoyle' shot - can be interpreted as a head with various horn-like protrusions and what could be an open mouth. A striking feature of this frame is that several frames immediately before and after it show the sky and the bottom of the boat from which the camera was suspended. This indicates that, in a lake apparently devoid of strong currents, the camera had been violently displaced through some 70 degrees of arc from two minutes before until three minutes after the photograph was taken.

The second striking 1975 photograph - the head, neck and body shot - shows what may be the head, neck and front part of the body of an animal with two appendages. This photograph certainly fits the evidence of many sightings which report a long neck and a small head, but the definition in the picture makes it inconclusive to many zoologists. The Gargoyle is, zoologically speaking, so unlike anything which might be expected that almost any alternative possibility is welcomed by the sceptic. One spokesman from the British Museum (Natural History) suggested a dead horse's head, another a dead stag's head and others who have seen and examined the picture have suggested driftwood which looks vaguely like an animal, parts of a Viking ship, or a discarded model for a film.

The last two can be immediately dismissed. Forestry Commission officials who have been consulted doubt that logs or waterlogged timber of that size could be floating around in midwater, while Mr Hyde, of the Princes Risborough Laboratory (formerly the Forest Research Laboratory) has said that 'most waterlogged logs sink, full stop.' However, it may be worth conducting further research on this subject so as to determine whether such logs could be confusing the issue.

My personal view is that the new evidence taken with the old, suggests there are indeed large animals in Loch Ness. My own guess, from ALL the reports is that they might look rather like plesiosaurs. - Sir Peter Scott

ASSIGNMENT ⑦

by Ronald Binns

OTTER ON LAND

The power of the picture.

Look at the large photograph. What does it suggest?
Can you always trust photographs?

ASSIGNMENT ⑧

Make a list of all the information you have read
that suggests Nessie exists; then find information
that suggests it does not. Having studied all the
evidence, present a talk to the class giving your
reasons for believing or not believing in the Loch
Ness Monster.

ASSIGNMENT 9

xamine all the evidence given that suggests Nessie xists. Design a leaflet that both persuades people hat Nessie is real and encourages them to visit the)rumnadrochit Exhibition Centre. Choose a heading that suggests that Nessie is no longer a myth or a legend.

ASSIGNMENT 10

Either

'Anyone who believes in the Loch Ness Monster must be crackers. I bet they believe in Unicorns and fairies at the bottom of the garden and dragons and ghosts!!' Giving reasons explain whether you think a Loch Ness Monster exists or not. Do you think that people who believe in the Loch Ness Monster are likely to believe in fairies, dragons and ghosts as this writer suggests?

or

It can never be proved that there are no large animals in Loch Ness, except by draining the loch. Do you think the question is important enough to go to those lengths?

INFORMATION WAS OBTAINED FROM:

- The Natural History Museum London.
- The National Museum of Scotland. Edinburgh.
- The Loch Ness Exhibition Centre, Drumnadrochit, Scotland.
- The International Society of Cryptozoologists.

CHAPTER 5

ASSIGNMENT ①

Study carefully *Who Protects the Animals?* and *Cats Tortured To Find Cure For Backache.*

These articles use pictures to present their point of view.

1 Decide as a group why the pictures in each of the extracts have been used. What are the motives behind them?

2 In the opening chapter you were told that pictures can have a powerful effect on a reader. What effect do these have on you?

- In the article *Who Protects the Animals* why are the people presented the way they are?
- Does the way they are dressed influence you? In what way?
- How does the picture of the cat featured in the newspaper article make you feel?
- Many articles use pictures. Always try to work out *why* they are there.

Who Protects the Animals?

Animals and the law

From 1987 the Animals (Scientific Procedures) Act says that the **project,** the **researcher** and the **premises** all need a licence.

Certificated premises.

I am the project director, I manage the project and hold the project licence which may last up to five years.

I am the Home Office Minister I issue all project licences. I make sure that only necessary research takes place. I will not give a project licence which allows cats, dogs, primates or horses to be used unless I am sure that rodents (rats and mice) will not do instead. I will only allow the use of cats and dogs which have been specially bred by registered breeders. I can protect any animal if I so choose.

I am a veterinary adviser, I make sure the animals are healthy and well.

I am an animal curator (I may be a vet), I make sure the animals live in good conditions.

Animal procedures committee: chairman and at least 12 members, including a lawyer, at least half of whom have had experience of research.

I am a pharma-cologist, I hold a personal licence.

I am a trained animal technician, I conduct procedures on animals. I hold a personal licence.

We are a statutory committee (that is, appointed under the law) appointed for four years. We advise the Home Office Ministers. The inspectors inform us, but we can make our own enquiries too. We will report annually to the Home Secretary on the use of animals in science during the previous year.

We inspectors help the Home Office Ministers. We are doctors or vets.

A **Regulated Procedure** is any experimental or other scientific procedure, applied to a protected animal, which may have the effect of causing that animal pain, suffering, distress or lasting harm.

I can have an animal put down, or stop an experiment if the animal is suffering. I shall probably call on your site at least 12 or 15 times a year and check that you are worthy of your licences.

Some of the animals that are protected

Source: C. R. Hobson

13

Horror experiments at top university

CATS TORTURED TO FIND CURE FOR BACKACHE

Pets die in lab hell

THOUSANDS of pet cats are being tortured to death in horrific university experiments to find a cure for human backache.

The helpless creatures die screaming in harrowing agony - crippled, mutilated and brain damaged by a series of barbaric tests.

The sadistic, secret research is centred at the University of California in Los Angeles, home to some of America's brightest young brains.

The scandal is being ignored. Top officials of the US government which has ploughed millions of dollars into the hush-hush horror, even deny that the animals suffer any pain.

But The People can reveal exclusive today the full catalogue of cruelty inflicted by laboratory scientists.

We have obtained gruesome pictures of the cats' hell which will shock the world.

CRUSHED

Peaches is one pathetic victim . . . . 15 months old and fully conscious but in the last throes of life.

His back is crushed and fur is shorn. A fearsome electrode has been drilled fully into his head. Five more are planted beneath the wounds crisscrossing his shaven skin.

He has just suffered twin blasts of hot air to the back and intense electric shocks to his paws and tail. He is in for 119 more.

They call it the "fear test." The current is recorded on an electronic graph as it passes through the cat's tortured nerve cells in his cage at UCLA's spinal research unit.

Doctors monitored Peaches' reaction before and after he was given shocks - to check his heart rate, respiration and brain response.

Dynamo is another stomach churning sight.

The lovable white kitten had his back crushed with lead weights before electrodes and wires were embedded beneath his skin.

A thousand more like him will perish this year. Some are tiny kittens.

Others are fully grown tabbies which fetch £100

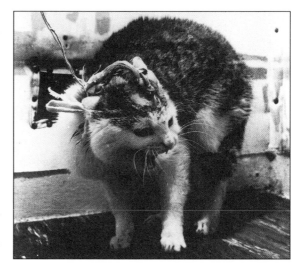

on a blooming black market.

A student's tip-off led Lifeforce, a leading antivivisection group, to carry out an eight-month undercover investigation.

The group,s founder, Peter Hamilton, said:

'Crippled animals die agonising deaths from what amounts to slow, systematic torture.

The surgeons give them names like Pegleg.

Then they break their spinal cords and plant electrodes in their heads. Kittens are dying also from burst bladders.

They have been "spinalised" - that is

medical jargon for it. It means the cats and kittens cannot empty their bladders.

Many are dying this way in excruciating pain.'

Scientists claim the experiments are vital in their quest to find a cure for back complaints.

But Mr Hamilton, 36 says most of the tests are unnecessary.

And Bill Dyer, president of the pressure group, Last Chance For Animals, told The People: "The link is never explained.

"The results of the tests have never been published."

Source: The People 12/7/87

ASSIGNMENT ②

Now look at the way all the articles are written, particularly *Cats Tortured to Find Cure for Backache*.

Remember the term 'emotive language' that you came across in *Foundation Skills*, pages 12–13. Re-read this information.

Study the language used in these articles and try to answer the following questions. Be ready to report back to the class.

Do any or all of the articles use emotive language? What is your mood likely to be after reading each article?

ASSIGNMENT ③

Look at the article *Who Protects the Animals*?

1. Why is all the information here presented by people talking about themselves and their qualifications?

2. How much do you learn from this article about what actually happens to the animals and what experiments are carried out?

3. What is the main purpose of the article?

ASSIGNMENT ④

Write a letter to the editor of the *People* (the newspaper which published *Cats Tortured To Find Cure For Backache*. Give your views on the article. You may not agree with the way the article was written or you may applaud it for its reporting of such a distasteful subject. You should comment on the style and content.

ASSIGNMENT ⑤

Imagine that you are a research scientist. You have received a letter from a pupil who wishes to know how your work benefits society and how the animals are protected. Write the reply a scientist might send.

ASSIGNMENT ⑥

Look at *Porton Down Torture Town* on page 56 and the advert *They Say Life Begins at Forty* produced by the Association of the British Pharmaceutical Industry. (This article appears in *Foundation Skills*, page 10.) Re-read the information that deals with fact and opinion in *Foundation Skills*, page 11.

ASSIGNMENT ⑦

Make a list of the reasons for and for not having animal experimentation. Use any information that you have found so far as well as any ideas you may already have. Put the list in two columns as this will help you with your later work.

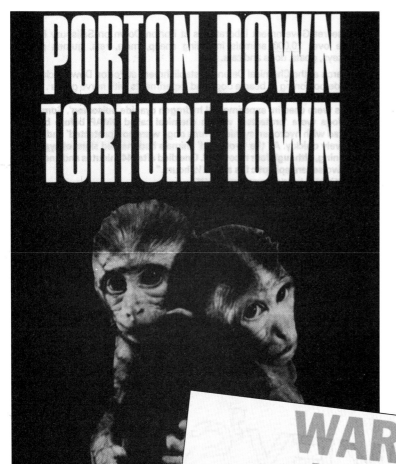

PORTON DOWN TORTURE TOWN

Source: Animal Aid

WARFARE
EXPERIMENTS

The search for ever more sophisticated ways of killing and maiming our fellow human beings continues, and as a direct result of this, rabbits, sheep, dogs, pigs, mice, guinea pigs, rats and monkeys are subjected to ballistic (conventional), chemical, nuclear and biological weaponry. This must be one of the most callous and inhuman uses of animals in British laboratories — This is warfare research: the most secret category of animal abuse, where the taxpayer funds 10,000 animals a year in laboratories where Crown immunity bypasses legislative control.

THEY SHOOT MONKEYS, DON'T THEY?

Ministry of Defence and scientific reports reveal how their Chemical Defence Establishment at Porton Down, Wiltshire, has tested riot control gas (CS gas) on animals; exposed monkeys and other animals to nerve gas; given dogs poisonous hydrogen cyanide; shot at live sheep with rubber and plastic bullets; shot monkeys through the head with ballbearings to investigate the effects of high velocity missiles; tested teargas (CN gas) on the eyes of conscious rabbits. Although we are told that the shooting experiments are carried out under anaesthetic, animals are sometimes allowed to recover immediately without treatment to their wounds.

CONDEMNED BY SURGEONS

Following an uproar in parliament over the shooting of monkeys, surgeons who have dealt with thousands of battle casualties at the Royal Victoria Hospital in Belfast, Northern Ireland said that these experiments are of no value in the treatment of human patients:

"How can they justify shooting animals — that aren't like humans anyway — just to see what the wounds are like. Nothing they could have learned at Porton Down could be of help to us here in Belfast."

NO POSSIBLE JUSTIFICATION

The defence of many of these experiments is that they are carried out for "defensive" reasons, but in fact results can always be used for "offensive" purposes (and who is to know?). The suffering which human beings inflict upon each other during the course of war is the responsiblity of the human species alone, and there can be no possible justification for the pain inflicted upon other animals to test ways of harming and destroying ourselves.

SLAUGHTER OF THE INNOCENT

At Porton Down, guinea pigs, rats and mice were forced to inhale CS riot control gas in order to see its poisonous effect. This is despite the fact that the gas has been in use for many years, and is well-known. The experiments took place for 1 hour every day, 5 days a week for up to 120 days. Many of the animals died during this period. "During the first month of the experiment 46% of the high dose group of guinea pigs perished". T.C. Marrs, et al, Archives of Toxicology, 1983, Vol.52, 183-198.

We can prove that experiments on animals are as misleading and unproductive as they are inhuman and sickeningly cruel. And warfare experiments are just the tip of the iceberg.

Source: NAVS

ASSIGNMENT ⑧

As a class read and study the information below, and *For All Our Sakes – Science Still Needs Animals* on page 58. Do these articles give you any new facts, opinions or information? If so, add them to your list of arguments in favour and opposed to animal experimentation.

ASSIGNMENT ⑨

Using the information that you have been given so far, write a page explaining how you feel about the use of animals in experiments. Always give reasons for your views. Be methodical as you will use this information in later work.

Deaths cause firm to withdraw drug

Painkillers are banned

Three die after taking new arthritis drug

Danger drugs taken off market

Two arthritis drugs banned by Ministry

Arthritis drug ban after 'seven deaths'

"But in part because of possible major differences in the responses to drugs of animals and man, the knowledge gained from studies in animals is often not pertinent to human beings, will almost certainly be inadequate and may even be misleading."
Arnold Welch, Yale University School of Medicine[5]

Source: Animal Aid

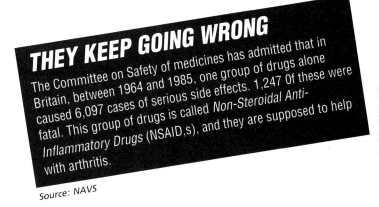

THEY KEEP GOING WRONG

The Committee on Safety of medicines has admitted that in Britain, between 1964 and 1985, one group of drugs alone caused 6,097 cases of serious side effects. 1,247 Of these were fatal. This group of drugs is called *Non-Steroidal Anti-Inflammatory Drugs (NSAID,s)*, and they are supposed to help with arthritis.

Source: NAVS

SAFETY-TESTED ON ANIMALS

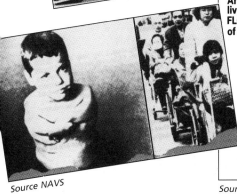

PENICILLIN — A useful antibiotic for people, but kills guinea pigs;
DIGITALIS — A heart drug for people, but causes dangerously high blood pressure in dogs;
CHLOROFORM — Anaesthetic for people, but poisonous to dogs;
MORPHINE — Calms people and rats but causes maniacal excitement in cats and mice.
ASPIRIN — Causes birth defects in rats, mice, monkeys, guinea pigs, cats, and dogs — but not in women.

ANIMAL TESTS FAIL TO PREDICT THE EFFECTS OF DRUGS WITH TRAGIC CONSEQUENCES: (All These Drugs Were Passed As Safe After Animal Tests).

ERALDIN, (ICI). Heart drug. Given to patients for 4 years before the horrific effects were identified, these include blindness, stomach troubles, joint pains and growths.
OPREN, (Dista/Eli Lilley). Non-steroidal anti-inflammatory drug (NSAID) — anti-arthritis. Withdrawn 1982. After more than 70 deaths and 3,500 others with serious side effects, including damage to skin, eyes, circulation, liver, kidneys.
FLOSINT, (Farmitalia). Another anti-inflammatory drug — Committee on Safety of Medicines had received reports of 217 adverse effects, including 7 deaths.

OSMOSIN, (Merck). Another NSAID. Withdrawn 1983. 650 had had side effects, and 20 died.
CHLORAMPHENICOL, (Parke Davis). Antibiotic, caused fatal blood disorders.
THALIDOMIDE, (Distillers). Sedative, used for morning sickness. About 10,000 birth defects world wide, and effects do not appear in most laboratory animals — so the human tragedy would probably still occur.

CLIOQUINOL (Ciba Geigy) Marketed as *entero-vioform,* caused 30 000 cases of paralysis and / or blindness and thousands of deaths in Japan: caused a new disease called SMON.

Source NAVS

Source: NAVS

For all our sakes– science still needs animals

- Faced with a severe illness or a critically ill relative, most people do not hesitate to have their doctor prescribe an effective medicine which will have been thoroughly tested, using animals.
- Even ardent anti-vivisectionists do not want to see their pets die if an animal-tested medicine can save their lives, or a vaccine prevent infection.
- Few would refrain from suing a manufacturer whose product disfigured or damaged them.
- At work, trade unionists and safety representatives demand safety data, based on animal studies, on substances they handle.

These are a few examples of the double standards we all apply but prefer to overlook.

However, we must ensure that those animals that *have* to be used are properly safeguarded.

Source: Research Defense Society

The facts

80 per cent of all animal experiments in Britain are for medical, dental or veterinary advancement. The remainder are for the protection of consumers or *workers in industry.*

In the past 50 years, medical research expenditure has increased, in real terms, 40-fold. In the same period the number of animal experiments had increased only 25-fold.

There has been a *steady decrease in animal experiments* in the last ten years.

We eat more than 400 million animals (cattle, pigs and poultry) each year in Britain–about 7 each.

Over 80% of all experiments involve rats or mice. Dogs account for only 0.25% and cats 0.14% of the total. The RSPCA kills very large numbers of unwanted cats and dogs every year–many times the number used in all UK laboratories.

ASSIGNMENT 10

Design a pamphlet either in favour or against animal experiments in which you include some of the ideas you have written above. Remember that a pamphlet is not just made up of visual artwork; it also uses *persuasive* language.

ASSIGNMENT 11

Bearing all that you have read in mind attempt the following.

Work with a partner and imagine you are both anti-vivisectionists. Design an advertisement for a well-known Sunday paper that exposes the dangers of research to the public. Try to make it eye-catching and Informative.

ASSIGNMENT 12

Imagine that you are a newspaper reporter. A group of anti-vivisectionists has broken into a laboratory and caused £5,000 worth of damage. They have also released four animals that were being treated successfully for cancer. Write an article that highlights the seriousness of the act and defends the use of animals in research studies.

This is worthy of a front page in a national newspaper. Remember that your story will need careful planning and must have an eye-catching title.

ASSIGNMENT ⓭

Either:

Imagine that you are listening to a radio documentary in which anti-vivisectionists and research scientists are discussing the use of animals in all types of research. Write the radio script of the argument that might take place between these two groups of people. You may wish to set this out as a conversation or in play form. Remember that all radio discussions of this kind will be led by the programme presenter.

This is not as straightforward as it may seem. Before you begin careful planning is needed. Make a list of the arguments made against research on one side of the page. Next to these on the opposite side list the counter argument to each point, *eg*:

AGAINST	**FOR**
Many animals die.	*Many more human beings and animals could benefit in the future*

Or:

'If I was forced to choose between my child or my dog I know which I would choose! What is the matter with our society? There are more societies to protect animals than there are to protect people. We condemn the use of animals in experiments but we eat meat and allow 600,000 dogs to be put down each year by the RSPCA. What a bunch of mindless hypocrites! If you wish to oppose research then stand up for your principles. You should be vegetarian, use toiletries and make-up that have not been tested on animals and refuse all medical treatments. How many of you have the guts to do that!!!'

Write an essay that explains how you feel about this writer's viewpoint. Discuss fully your own feelings about this issue.

INFORMATION WAS OBTAINED FROM:

- *Organisations opposed to research*
- BUAV. 16a Crane Grove, Islington, London N7 8LB.
- NAVS. 51 Harley Street, LONDON.
- Mobilisation for Laboratory Animals. As Above.
- ANIMAL AID. 7 Castle Street, Tonbridge, Kent.
- FRAME. (Fund for the Replacement of Animals in Research), Eastgate House, 34 Stoney Street, Nottingham NG1 1NB.
- Teachers for Animal Rights. 29 Lynwood Road, London SW17 8SB
- Youth for Animal Rights. Hillview, Chaffcombe, Nr Chard Somerset.
- Anglican Society for the Welfare of Animals. 10 Chester Avenue, Hawkenbury, Tunbridge Wells, Kent.
- Catholic Study Circle for Animal Welfare. 37 Onslow Gardens, South Woodford, London E18.
- *Organisations in favour of research*
- AMRIC. Animals in Medicines in Research Information Centre. 12 Whitehall, London SW1A 2DY.
- RESEARCH DEFENCE SOCIETY. Grosvenor Gardens House, Grosvenor Gardens, London SW1W 0BS.

C H A P T E R 6

euthanasia
euthanasia
euthanasia

A S S I G N M E N T ①

Read carefully the information given below.

We are God's children. Only he can decide to take our life. It is not ours to take.

I think legalising euthanasia is a good idea. Think of the problems it would solve – no old people, no handicapped babies and no compassion. Everything we could possibly want from a civilised society! Is this what we really desire – I hope not.

I agree with euthanasia in certain cases, after I had the experience of an acquaintance who choked to death after cancer of the neck. The poor man pleaded for weeks to his wife to be allowed to die.

I feel most strongly about euthanasia, having watched my dear husband dying with lung cancer and crying in agony. He told me one day: 'If I was an animal I could be put to sleep'.

Over the past twenty years, I have been living with a cancerous disease which is slowly poisoning the whole of my body, and I would like to have the right to choose when the time comes that I feel my endurance is at an end.

My grandmother died of cancer of the bowel. She took three weeks to die – three weeks full of the most appalling agony. In fact she was crying out for most of that time for the doctors to end her torment. In the end she was screaming in pain. Is it too much to ask for the right to die peacefully?

EUTHANASIA IS NOT THE ANSWER

The humanitarian and emotional reactions aroused in those observing someone severely disabled, diseased or dying are understandably distressing - particularly for the family.

Not knowing what to do or what to say to alleviate apparent suffering leads to frustrated helplessness. Some people go away, 'I can't bear to see him like this'

The suffering in so many cases is on the part of the beholder and not the patient.

It is a dreadful indictment of our medical services that one of the main arguments in favour of euthanasia is that so many people do die in physical and mental distress. But surely we do not have to kill the patient in order to kill the distress.

That many patients die with pain unrelieved or distressing symptoms untreated or inadequately treated is undeniable. The care of the terminally ill patient is all too often sadly mismanaged, and it is all the more sad because we have got the wherewithal, in medications and various therapies to give our patients significant, and in most cases complete relief from pain and discomfort.

Dr J Hanratty Medical Director St Joseph's Hospice.

The most obvious objection to euthanasia is that the choice to end someone's life would depend very often on the diagnosis of doctors. They are not always correct in this. Last year fourteen patients were admitted to St Joseph's having been diagnosed as suffering from advanced cancer - they were found to have no cancer at all or the cancer was in such an early stage that it was still amenable to treatment.

St Joseph's Hospice

Make a list of the reasons that are given in favour of euthanasia and against it in the quotations above.

ASSIGNMENT ❷

Look at the extract from *Whose Life Is It Anyway?*
Discuss and answer the following questions:

1 What reasons does Ken give for wishing to die?

2 In what way does the judge say Ken differs from a person whose heart is used in a transplant?

3 What argument does the judge put forward to try to dissuade Ken?

4 How does Ken answer the arguments?

5 What impression does the reader get of the doctors and hospital Ken is in?

6 As a group take the decision that the judge makes in this play. Give reasons for your answer.

WHOSE LIFE IS IT ANYWAY ?

JUDGE: Do you feel like answering some questions?
KEN: Of course.
JUDGE: Thank you.
KEN: You are too kind.
JUDGE: Not at all.
KEN: I mean it, I'd prefer it if you were a hanging judge.
JUDGE: There aren't any any more.
KEN: Society is now much more sensitive and humane?
JUDGE: You could put it that way.
KEN: I'll settle for that.
JUDGE: I would like you to take the oath. Dr Scott, his right hand please.
[Ken takes the oath.]
The consultant physician here has given evidence that you are not capable of making a rational decision.
KEN: He's wrong.
JUDGE: Why then do you think he came to that opinion?
KEN: He's a good doctor and won't let a patient die if he can help it.
JUDGE: He found that you were suffering from acute depression.
KEN: Is that surprising? I am almost totally paralysed. I'd be insane if I weren't depressed.
JUDGE: But there is a difference between being unhappy and being depressed in the medical sense.
KEN: I would have thought that my psychiatrist answered that point.
JUDGE: But surely wishing to die must be strong evidence that the depression has moved beyond a mere unhappiness into a medical realm?
KEN: I don't wish to die.
JUDGE: Then what is this case all about?
KEN: Nor do I wish to live at any price. Of course I want to live but as far as I am concerned, I'm dead already. I merely require the doctors to recognise the fact. I cannot accept this condition constitutes life in any real sense at all.
JUDGE: Certainly, you're alive legally.
KEN: I think I could challenge even that.
JUDGE: How?
KEN: Any reasonable definition of life must include the idea of its being self-supporting. I seem to remember something in the papers - when all the heart transplant controversy was on - about it being alright to take someone's heart if they require constant attention from respirators and so on to keep them alive.
JUDGE: There also has to be absolutely no brain activity at all. Yours is certainly working.
KEN: It is and sanely.
JUDGE: That is the question to be decided.
KEN: My Lord, I am not asking anyone to kill me. I am only asking to be discharged from this hospital.
JUDGE: It comes to the same thing.
KEN: Then that proves my point; not just the fact that I will spend the rest of my life in hospital, but that whilst I am here, everything is geared just to keeping my brain

active, with no real possibility of it ever being able to to direct anything. As far as I can see, that is an act of deliberate cruelty.
JUDGE: Surely it would be more cruel if society let people die, when it could, with some effort, keep them alive.
KEN: No, not more cruel, just as cruel.
JUDGE: Then why should the hospital let you die - if it is just as cruel?
KEN: The cruelty doesn't reside in saving someone or allowing them to die. It resides in the fact that the choice is removed from the man concerned.
JUDGE: But a man who is very desperately depressed is not as capable of making a reasonable choice.
KEN: As you said, my Lord, that is the question to be decided.
JUDGE: Alright. You tell me why it is a reasonable choice that you decided to die.
KEN: It is a question of dignity. Look at me here. I can do nothing, not even the basic primitive functions. I cannot even urinate. I have a permanent catheter attached to me. Every few days my bowels are washed out. Every few hours two nurses have to turn me over or I would rot away from bedsores. Only my brain functions unimpaired but even that is futile because I can't act on any conclusions it comes to. This hearing proves that. Will you please listen.
JUDGE: I am listening.
KEN: I choose to acknowledge the fact that I am in fact dead and I find the hospital's persistent effort to maintain this shadow of life an indignity and it's inhumane.
JUDGE: But wouldn't you agree that many people with appalling physical handicaps have overcome them and lived essentially creative, dignified lives.
KEN: Yes. I would, but the dignity starts with their choice. If I choose to live, it would be appalling if society killed me. If I choose to die, it is equally appalling if society keeps me alive.
JUDGE: I cannot accept that it is undignified for society to devote resources to keeping someone alive. Surely it enhances that society.
KEN: It is not undignified if the man wants to stay alive, but I must restate that the dignity starts with his choice. Without it, it is degrading because technology has taken over from human will. My Lord, if I cannot be a man, I do not wish to be a medical achievement. I'm fine... I am fine.
JUDGE: It's alright. I have no more questions.
[the Judge stands up and walks to the window. He thinks a moment.]
JUDGE: This is most unusual case. Before I make a judgement I want to state that I believe all the parties have acted in good faith.

from WHOSE LIFE IS IT
ANYWAY? by Brian Clark.

ASSIGNMENT ③

Imagine that the event from *Whose Life Is It Anyway?* occurred in real life. A television documentary involving a live discussion between the judge,

representatives from EXIT (a group in favour of euthanasia) and doctors follows the event. Script the documentary programme. Include as many arguments that were used in the extract as possible as well as some of your own.

■ Refer again to the play and look at the list of reasons you made earlier.

WORSE THAN DEATH?

ASK people what they would like to happen to them if they should have the misfortune to suffer from senile dementia and many of them say that they hope they will have the good luck to get a sharp attack of pneumonia - and that their doctor will not do anything foolish like trying to treat it. Or that someone will have the kindness to slip something into their tea. So why is it that the NHS spends a sizeable chunk of its budget trying to prolong the existence of patients suffering from senile dementia?

It is probable that most of those who suffer severely from it are unaware of their predicament, as they are unaware of practically everything else that makes human existence meaningful. The suffering falls chiefly on their nearest and dearest, contemplating the wreck of someone they once loved and knowing that before becoming demented, the victim would have given a great deal to secure an early and dignified end to his vegetoid existence were it possible.

What phrase shall we use to describe the fate of a man, a former cabinet minister, who suffered a very severe stroke several years ago? As well as paralysing him on one side he cannot speak, read, and write, although he is able to understand what is said to him.

There are two particularly cruel ironies about his present state. The first is that he used

to be a brilliant communicator, making crisp and memorable speeches without notes. Now, his vocabulary is limited to three or four words which he cannot always use appropriately.

The second irony is that until his stroke, both he and his wife had been active members of the Voluntary Euthanasia Society, and his wife still is. It was an issue about which he felt strongly and I know exactly what he thought about the utter pointlessness, for him, of being kept alive in the sort of condition he now has to endure. From his answers to questions it is very evident that he would dearly like to be put out of his misery. He would willingly take a lethal overdose and it would be perfectly legal for him to do so, but for his family to place the necessary drugs on his bedside table would be a serious and imprisonable offence.

And since the police seized the membership list of the Voluntary Euthanasia Society around the time of his stroke and have since taken a special interest in deaths involving its members, they fear the consequences.

The courts are usually quite sympathetic in these situations ("...understand your feelings... no ulterior motive... quite accept that you loved him dearly... nevertheless court cannot ignore... two years probation") but they are unpredictable and sometimes feel the need to make an example.

A member of the House of Lords is considering introducing a bill which, among other things, would decriminalise the altruistic and compassionate assisting of suicide by family or physicians in such cases. It would also permit people to appoint, while in good health, friends or relations who would be empowered to speak and instruct on their behalf, in matters of treatment, if they themselves were no longer able to do so.

There is certainly a trend in several countries towards allowing patients a greater say in the timing and manner of their dying, but this is mainly evident in cases of terminal or rapidly progressive illness, and anyway, it remains to be seen whether the trend has reached Westminster.

One of this man's frustrations is that his condition is evidently far from terminal. Like Karen Quinlan in America - still nominally alive though cerebrally dead 10 years after her life support machines were switched off in the hope that she would follow suit - he could go on like this for years. Unlike Karen Quinlan, he knows that.

Although his condition is an emotional strain on his family, it is not a financial one. They are not short of money and he is being treated in an NHS geriatric unit with loving care.

His doctors are not even officiously striving to keep him alive. A few months ago, he had an attack of pneumonia

and the doctors, with his enthusiastic approval, withheld antibiotics. (This is passive euthanasia and the practice is very wide-spread.) Since in most cases the patients are in no position to say whether or not they wish to be treated, it is also decidedly involuntary euthanasia. It is just as illegal as the voluntary, active kind.

Here, then, lies the living body of a man who used to be one of this country's leading and most honoured citizens. Both before and since his stroke he has made it as clear as he possibly can that he does not wish to continue living like this.

In a generally free country, he is denied the one freedom that matters most to him at the moment: the freedom to obtain assistance in ending his life in dignity when he is no longer in a position to end it himself.

There are those who talk about the dangers of making such things legal, of the possibility of mistakes. Yet the freedom to make mistakes which mainly affect ourselves is one of the most basic freedoms of all. We permit it, in practice, to the sort of suicide whose death often causes great distress to others.

In an age when more people than ever live rather well, is it not strange that so many people have to die rather badly?

Dr Brewer is a consultant psychiatrist.

Source: The Sunday Times 18/9/84

ASSIGNMENT ④

Look at the article *Worse than Death?* on page 63. Read the following questions, and discuss your answers.

1 What is senile dementia?

2 What do you learn about the cabinet minister mentioned?

3 Why can't his family help him?

4 What sort of pressure does his illness put on his family?

5 Look at the paragraph beginning 'A member of the House of Lords . . .'. What safeguards are suggested for old people here?

6 Is the man discussed here terminally ill?

7 Are doctors sympathetic to the man's wish to die? Give reasons for your answer.

8 Look at the extract and particularly the last two paragraphs. What arguments does the writer use for allowing euthanasia?

9 Are you in favour of or against this man being allowed to die? Give reasons for your answer.

10 Look carefully at the passage. Pick out the emotive words the writer uses to emphasise his case. Explain how these words affect the reader.

11 How does the position of the cabinet minister in this article differ from Ken's position in *Whose Life Is It Anyway?*

ASSIGNMENT ⑤

Write a page on euthanasia considering what you have read so far. Are you for it, against it, or do you have mixed feelings? Give reasons for your views.

ASSIGNMENT ⑥

At the end of the article *Worse than Death?* the author referred to the dangers of legalising euthanasia. Read *Three out of Four Back Mercy Killing* then in your group discuss and write down what some of these dangers might be.

- People say that such treatment of handicapped children is similar to Hitler's treatment of handicapped people in Nazi Germany. Would you agree with this?
- Are there dangers in allowing children to die in this way?
- Is there a difference between euthanasia of a new-born handicapped baby and the abortion of a healthy child?
- Are both legal?
- Should parents and doctors be able to make such decisions?
- What rights does the child have? Should they be protected?

THREE OUT OF FOUR BACK MERCY KILLING

THREE out of four people are in favour of legalising mercy killing, a survey revealed yesterday.

Half of those questioned support euthanasia provided it is requested by a patient who is critically ill and in pain.

A further 23 per cent favour death on request regardless of the severity of the illness or pain.

Around a third of those who support euthanasia believe that relatives should be allowed to ask for it on behalf of a patient unable to communicate.

by CHRIS MIHILL
Medical Correspondent

Mori interviewed 1,808 adults after being commissioned by two pressure groups opposed to euthanasia, Doctors Who Respect Human Life and the Human Rights Society.

The groups called the results "frightening" and "the start of the slippery slope towards the gas chambers".

Forty per cent of those questioned felt that if a patient had asked for euthanasia, a doctor should be obliged to carry it out.

But 44 per cent felt that if mercy killing was legal, patients would be frightened to go into hospital.

At a London press conference to publicise the survey, terminal care expert Professor Robin Hull insisted that with modern methods nearly every patient could be assured of relief from pain.

He claimed that patients often requested death because they were suffering from depression which could be treated.

Dr Peggy Norris, secretary of Doctors Who Respect Human Life, said: "The extent of public ignorance about modern pain control represents a danger to the lives of the sick and helpless.

"The results of this poll are frightening."

She said if euthanasia is legalised, objections on moral grounds could mean "poor job prospects for doctors who weren't willing to kill their patients on request. This is a recipe for a nightmare".

Elderly

Dr Norris, a Liverpool GP, claimed that in Holland, where euthanasia is practised, some elderly people have to be counselled before they go in to hospital because they are frightened they will be "put down."

The British Medical Association is carrying out its own review of doctors' attitudes towards mercy killing.

Source: T ay 24/3/88

ASSIGNMENT

ead the article *A Baby's Right to Live or Die* and he SPUC advertisement on pages 66–67. Discuss as group the contents of the newspaper article. ecide whether you are in favour of euthanasia in hese cases or not and give reasons.

ote: *SPUC is the Society for the Protection of the nborn Child.*

ASSIGNMENT 8

nagine that *A Baby's Right to Live or Die?* has just een printed in your local paper. Write a letter in esponse to it either opposing or supporting uthanasia in these cases.

ASSIGNMENT 9

o you think there are any differences between uthanasia for adults who are in great pain or virually helpless and euthanasia for new-born handipped babies? If so, do you feel the same way bout both types of euthanasia?

I'm writing this message with my foot.

I live a very full and active life
Even though I am severely handicapped.
I was severely handicapped when I was born.
The kind of baby that is sometimes left to
die these days.
I believe they call it "mercy killing."
Mercifully — I was allowed to live.

Marilyn Carr

MARILYN CARR FORMERLY INDEPENDENT PRO LIFE CANDIDATE FOR CROYDON NORTH WEST

A great many severely handicapped people, and many parents of equally handicapped children, are alarmed at the growing acceptance of the 'mercy killing' of handicapped babies.
They accept that the motives are usually humane – but, understandably, believe these motives are misguided.
If you share our concern at this medical trend, please write and give us your support. Handicap Division, S.P.U.C., 7 Tufton Street, London SW1P 3QN. Tel: 01-222 5845.

Source: SPUC

ASSIGNMENT ⑩

Design a leaflet that supports or opposes euthanasia. It needs to contain information that is informative and persuasive.

ASSIGNMENT ⑪

As a class debate this issue. Decide whether you agree or disagree with the following quotation and structure your arguments around it.

'Someone once said that a civilized society is one that cares for its old people and protects the young and weak. What type of society are we when we suggest killing off our old and putting our young handicapped children down? Out of their misery! I suggest it is for our benefit we would suggest such a thing – not theirs!'

INFORMATION WAS OBTAINED FROM:

- The Voluntary Euthanasia Society. 13 Prince of Wales Terrace, London W8 5PG.
- The Medical Director. St Joseph's Hospice, Mare Street, Hackney, London SW1V 1PD.
- The Catholic Truth Society. P.O. Box 422. 38-40 Eccleston Square, London.
- LIFE, National Headquarters. 118-120 Warwick Street, Leamington Spa, Warwickshire CV32 4QY.
- SPUC. (Society for the Protection of the Unborn Child) 7 Tufton Street, Westminster SW1 3QN.

A baby's right to live - or die

CHRISTINE DOYLE,
OUR MEDICAL CORRESPONDENT, REPORTS ON THE MORAL, ETHICAL AND LEGAL DILEMMAS HIGHLIGHTED BY THE RECENT COURT RULING.

AT LEAST four surgeons at the Hospital for Sick Children in London refused to operate to save the life of a Down's Syndrome baby when requested to do so a week ago by a social services director, despite strong objections to the operation by the baby's parents.

The case has caused an ethical storm, with the anti-abortion Life group inflaming the controversy by calling on hospital workers of all kinds to report attitudes in their hospital to allowing newborn malformed babies to die. The group has already sent notes on a number of 'incidents' to the Director of Public Prosecutions.

The baby, born more than two weeks ago at Queen Charlotte's Hospital in West London, had an intestinal blockage, which rapidly proves fatal, if nothing is done - absorption of food is impossible.

After much anguish the parents were convinced that it was in the child's best interests to allow nature to take its course. But the Hammersmith Social Services director head of the case, thought otherwise. Mr. David Plank, who had a mongol child had the baby made a ward of the court.

When the surgeons refused to operate he returned to the judge who gave the child into his safekeeping, and asked him to order an operation. The judge then refused to do so. Undeterred, Mr. Plank went to the Appeal Court, where with time running out for the child's life, an operation was ordered.

This case marks the entry of the law in Britain into an ethical area with few hard and fast guidelines. A Times leading article argued that 'it must almost inevitably be right for the court to come down on the side of life wherever there is a division of opinion among those directly concerned so strong that the issue is brought before it.'

Subsequent debate among doctors, social workers, parents of children with Down's syndrome (mongolism) and others show however that the dilemma is more acute than ever with the Life group's activities creating an atmosphere of deep suspicion and mistrust. In a case which is now subjudice, a consultant paediatrician is accused of the murder of a three-day-old mongol child baby.

Where does a humane, caring society draw the line at permitting nature to take its course? Does the Appeal Court judges' decision provide a dividing line which we must accept for the future? The actual practice of many doctors in this country strongly suggests that the judges' opinion in this case should not be regarded as a precedent.

Every day babies are born with malformations requiring a life or death decision. One paediatrician said that he had been involved in such a decision about once a week for many years. In the case of a 'monster' or children so mentally or physically

Craig Seton decided Rebecca should have an operation.

handicapped it may be plainly obvious that an operation would 'condemn' them to life.

Relief of suffering rather than saving life whatever the cost is the generally acceptable guideline for these children. If feeding such babies may produce a lingering and painful death, it is sometimes thought better to provide simply sugar and water and sedation. Some doctors, conscious of the distress this causes to everyone concerned, offer milk but it may make little difference to the outcome.

At one time modern surgery and intensive care for spina-bifida babies 'salvaged' many who either died within a year, or were condemned to severely crippled lives in institutions. In the 1970's Professor John Lorber, head of paediatrics at the Children's Hospital in Sheffield, drew up his now well-known guidelines which resulted in many fewer operations, much to the relief of both parents and medical workers. These guidelines helped doctors to predict the degree of paralysis, incontinence, hunchback and possible retardation.

One baby in every 500 is a Down's baby, but there are no similar guidelines, and many are on the borderline when it comes to making predictions about their future. Some 10 per cent have a fatal intestinal blockage, and others may have heart defects.

A paediatrician in the South West told me that in 10 years he had never come across a case where the decision had been taken to operate on a fatal intestinal blockage in a Down's baby. He says: 'It is where I draw the line, and would if my own baby was affected. Over years of discussions with doctors, parents and others, I think it is the point where you find most people say "I agree with you".'

But what if a Down's baby did not have any extra defects and became acutely ill in the first days of life with, say, a severe infection? Would he treat the baby to save life? Depending upon the parents' wishes and the individual clinical circumstances this doctor said that he would not treat the baby. Many of his colleagues also believed this to be an ethical way to proceed. But he would make a different decision if the baby were older than a few days.

He and many others - parents of Down's children among them - point out the hypocrisy of a society which aborts normal babies for social reasons, strives to discover handicap

during pregnancy so that a legal abortion may take place, but which may then not let a new-born mongol baby with a lethal malformation die naturally.

In one intensive care baby unit in the London area, nurses and doctors repeatedly save the life of virtually helpless premature normal babies. But the consultant paediatrician in charge feels so strongly about operating on seriously handicapped babies with a lethal defect that he would refer the child to another hospital if the parents insisted on an operation.

Most, though not all of his colleagues agreed with him. He described what happened in three cases where a mongol baby had a lethal intestinal obstruction.

In the first, the parents did not want to proceed with the operation, but felt they should consult their Catholic priest who advised that they shold consent to an operation. The doctor, however, then advised a 'second opinion' from their bishop, who on learning that in this case the chance of successful operation was 30 per cent told the parents: 'It is for God to take life, not a surgeon." The operation did not take place and the baby died.

The second case was a very premature baby weighing about three pounds in whom Down's syndrome was not recognised initially. The operation took place but the baby survived for only 18 months, and spent much time in hospital with a conjenital heart defect

The third was the mongol baby of a doctor's family where the parents initially said that they did not want the operation to take place. But after a family debate they felt 'guilty' and changed their minds. The baby died 12 hours after the operation from natural causes.

The paediatrician commented: 'These and other cases make me absolutely convinced that it is meddlesome to perform surgery on babies who are such operative risks.'

On the other hand, many parents have in the past week testified to the love and fulfilment that Down's children can enjoy, though not all - Mr. Plank among them - have had to take a life or death decision at birth. Craig Seton, a Times journalist whose five-year-old daughter Rebecca has Down's syndrome, did have to decide. He is absolutely convinced that he and his wife were correct to consent to an operation to remove an intestinal blockage, even though it was made clear that the surgeon would not proceed if they did not wish it.

But the entry of the courts into the debate has left him as confused as anybody else: 'I cannot condemn the parents for not wanting an operation, but at the same time I think it is marvellous that the courts did give this child the right to live.'

One paediatrician probably echoes the feeling of many parents and doctors when he says, 'I believe it better if the courts did not get involved. I think all of us, parents and doctors, have to work within the framework of the law, conscious that we may be operating close to the edge of it. In the past I think the law has respected our dilemma.'

Source: The Observer 16/8/81

CHAPTER 7

Creatures that look like the Yeti have been sighted in other parts of the world. To the inhabitants of these countries they have names other than Yeti – Sasquatch and Big Foot, for instance.

AN ABOMINABLE SAGA UNFOLDS

by Peter Gilman

YETI FEVER is spreading among the mountaineering fraternity again. Climbers returning from the Himalayas, and others preparing to depart are once more talking about the half-human, half-beast which supposedly inhabits the kingdom of snows.

Tony Wooldridge, just back from the Garwhal Himalayas, says he found *"yeti-like tracks"*, the size of human footprints, at 13,500 ft. Chris Bonington, veteran of five Everest expeditions who is planning to climb in the Menlungtse region, where several tracks have been found, says: *"I take the yeti seriously. I think there is something there."*

But is there any scientific basis for such beliefs? A controversy currently preoccupying the climbing world suggests that the crucial evidence may be more fragile than most people suspect - and may even be a hoax. The surviving key witness, whom we contacted last week, denies that.

The yeti acquired its greatest credibility from an episode during the Everest reconnaissance expedition of 1951. (The triumphal first ascent by Hillary and Tenzing followed two years later). While negotiating the Menlung glacier, the mountaineer Eric Shipton took two photographs, widely reproduced since.

One showed a line of tracks heading across the snow, with Shipton's partner, the young climbing doctor, Mike Ward standing beside them.

The second showed a close-up of a single giant footprint, with a curious array of toes: two large ones on the right, a gap, and three smaller ones on the left. Measured against Ward's ice-axe, it was 13 inches by eight - the size of a gorilla's foot, or a large bear's.

Since no known creature could have made such tracks, Shipton's pictures attracted wide publicity. They were published in the Times under the heading *"Footprints of the Abominable Snowman"* and were exhibited at the Natural History Museum.

They also spawned a new science, cryptozoology. One authority, Professor Bernard Heuvelmans, produced imaginative drawings of the Shipton yeti: a cross between a bear and an ape, which used its two big toes to grip steep rock.

Sightings of footprints have followed thick and fast ever since. Many were almost certainly made by more mundane creatures-monkeys or snow leopards. But nobody has yet explained the Shipton footprint in conventional terms.

From time to time, however there have been whispers that the crucial Shipton footprint might not be all it seemed. An early sceptic was Sir Edmund Hillary; he suggested that it may have been *"enhanced"*. Then the biologist Professor John Napier declared he could not imagine what kind of beast could have made the print. since the ball of its foot appeared concave instead of convex.

Most recently, the mountaineering historian Audrey Salkeld, a fellow of the Royal Geographical Society, has gone further. Writing in *"Mountain"* magazine, she suggests that the crucial footprint may have been *"cooked"* - with its toes added, perhaps, by Shiptons knuckles. Mrs Salkeld believes that it may have been an example of Shipton's well known *"puckish sense of humour:*, and cites two previous examples.

Further doubts arise from the curious way Shipton changed his story. At first he implied that his two key photographs - the trail in the snow and the footprint with toes - were taken from the same set of tracks.

But when Professor Napier pointed out there were discrepancies between them, Shipton apparently clarified the matter: they were not made by the same creature after all, but represented two sets of tracks found close to each other.

Since Shipton died in 1977, the best witness to events on the Menlung glacier is his partner, Dr Mike Ward, now a consultant at a London hospital.

Dr Ward is emphatic that the crucial footprint *"was not a hoax"*. Yet in some ways his comments deepen the mystery.

Dr Ward says that he has always tried to make it clear that there were two sets of tracks. Yet in his autobiography, published in 1972, he, too, referred to only one set. Last week Dr Ward provided new information about the second set of tracks. He said they formed part of a trail, 50 yards from the first set, which he and Shipton had followed for *"about a quarter of a mile-and it continued on down."*

Why did Shipton photograph only a single footprint of the second trail? *"He was not very scientifically minded,"* Dr Ward said.

Dr Ward believes that, whereas the first set of prints may have been made by a sheep or goat, he has *"no idea"* what caused the second.

Professor Napier now expresses a more forthright view than hitherto. *"I never believed that footprint,"* he says. *"It's so phoney."*

Audrey Salkeld guesses that it was a joke that went too far. Chris Bonington, meanwhile, is keeping an open mind. But, if he does find a yeti around Menlungtse, he will be strongly tempted to keep the news to himself. *"If the yeti has survived all this time, you hope it can go on surviving,"* he says.

Much better, he adds, to leave it in peace.

Source: The Daily Telegraph 12/5/86

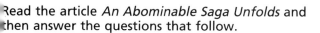

Read the article *An Abominable Saga Unfolds* and then answer the questions that follow.

1 What did Tony Wooldridge find in the Himalayas?

2 Using information from the passage explain what you think the Yeti looks like.

3 Why do you think the word abominable is used in the headline?

4 Read the passage again carefully. According to the writer why was Eric Shipton so important?

5 What does Chris Bonington say about the existence of a Yeti?

6 What does Chris Bonington say should be done if a Yeti is found? Giving your reasons explain whether you agree with him or not?

7 What evidence is given in the passage to suggest a Yeti exists?

8 What evidence is given in the passage to deny the existence of the Yeti?

9 Divide the people in the passage into those who believe, those who are likely to believe, and those who do not believe in the Yeti's existence.

10 Giving reasons explain whether you think the Yeti exists or not. You do not have to confine your answer to the passage.

Army joker dreamed up spooky beast of the Himalayas

I INVENTED YETI, SAYS ABOMINABLE CONMAN

THE Abominable Snowman never existed –
He was invented by British Army officer back in 1916.

Lieutenant "Daddy" Newman made up the Yeti myth for spooky stories he wrote in an Indian newspaper.

The new evidence is published in the Punjab Frontier Force Association's magazine.

It quotes a letter from Lieutenant Newman to a brother officer, which reveals how the Abominable Conman dreamed up the Abominable Snowman.

FIGMENT

The letter says: "It's a figment of my imagination, old boy.

"The Tibetans believe in ghosts which they call Yetis - and so I have invented the A.S."

Lieutenant-Colonel Ivor Edwards-Stuart, editor of the magazine, said: "There is no doubt in my mind Newman was speaking the truth.

Both Newman and the officer who received the letter are now dead.

Last night Yeti-hunting mountaineer Chris Bonington slammed the new evidence.

He stormed: "This is nonsense. The Yeti DOES exist - there's too much evidence.

"Too many sensible people have seen the creature. It's an ape-like beast, with long reddish hair.

TRACKS

Chris led a team through the Himalayan foothills this year, searching for the Yeti.

"We found some fascinating tracks in the snow," he said.

by Peter Bond

ASSIGNMENT ②

Read the article *I Invented the Yeti says Abominable Conman.*

You are going to make a tape recording of the interviews quoted in the article. Choose who is to play the reporter, Chris Bonington and Lieutenant-Colonel Ivor Edwards-Stuart. You should prepare as well as you are able before-hand. Remember the quotations used in the article will have been part of a much longer conversation. Try to sound as you think these characters might.

ASSIGNMENT ③

The first two articles, *An Abominable Saga Unfolds* and *I Invented the Yeti says Abominable Conman,* were both about the Yeti. Write about one page explaining how they are similar/different in their style of writing.

Look at:
- The content of each. How does it differ? Does it set out to persuade you to believe or disbelieve?
- The use of pictures.
- Number of words.
- Use of language.
- Use of reliable witness reports.
- Does it explore all possibilities?

DID I SEE THE YETI ?

THE GREAT EXPEDITION, 1988
Report No 4 from the front

Top TV film man tells of his amazing encounter on a Himalayan mountain

IAIN WALKER
reports from the
Menlungtse Valley, Tibet

Pictures by
DAVID O'NEILL

AN ASTONISHING ENCOUNTER WITH A MYSTERIOUS CREATURE, 15,000 FEET UP A MOUNTAIN, HAS GIVEN THE CHRIS BONINGTON EXPEDITION AN EXCITING NEW CLUE IN THE HUNT FOR THE HIMALAYAN YETI.

BBC TV film director John-Paul Davidson has told me how he was followed for 15 minutes by a large black animal which appeared to stand on two legs and peer at him from a ridge.

At first he thought it was a bear - then he spotted a series of footsteps in the snow.

And when he examined them, it was clear they were far too big for any of the three species of bear known to exist in this part of Southern Tibet.

They measured 15in long and 6in wide... even larger than a man's footsteps. But because there was a blizzard raging, fresh snow had softened the contours and no toes were discernible.

Cautious

Yet one thing was certain whatever had made the tracks appeared to have been moving in huge 4ft bounds.

Davidson, 34, has wide experience making BBC TV natural history films. He studied anthropology at post-graduate level at university and is married to Magnus Magnusson's daughter, Margaret, who is also a BBC producer.

All his training has taught him to be cautious before making definitive judgements... yet he cannot explain away what he saw while clambering after those tracks on a 50 degree precipice.

Davidson took a series of pictures, of the tracks and of the creature watching him. But he had only an automatic-focus 35 mm camera. And because the creature was above him and 400 yards away, he is not sure what the final results will be.

Unexpected

Could it have been the Yeti? John-Paul admits it *could* because the tracks are too big for the Himalayan black, blue or brown bear - and no other known animal species could have made them.

But it is still far from the conclusive proof the Bonington expedition needs.

As with previous sightings of the legendary half-man, half-ape creature, the encounter happened unexpectedly.

The BBC's internationally-respected Natural History Unit is making an hour-long TV documentary about the search for the Yeti, which we have reported exclusively in The Mail on Sunday since March.

Davidson and his film team took an afternoon's exploratory stroll with Dr Charles Clarke, a consultant neurologist at Bart's Hospital, London, who is acting as the team's scientific officer.

But as they were collecting droppings from various animal species for later laboratory examination, they spotted an interesting series of tracks high up a steep snow gully in the side of the mountain.

Davidson told me: *"I suddenly noticed, about 300 feet or so above me, a curious black shape under a bolder. I stared at it for about two or three minutes - then it moved*

Cut off by the snow, I felt my heart racing

higher up the ridge.

'My first thought - almost halfheartedly - was about the Yeti, but as I looked more carefully I thought again about a bear.

'It reminded me of the large stuffed bears, standing up menacingly on two legs which you see at any natural history museum.

Attack

'It was snowing quite heavily at the time... and I don't mind admitting that my heart was racing. I was pretty frightened and totally alone, cut off from my colleagues by the impending blizzard.

And I knew that some of the Himalayan bears have the reputation of attacking a man.

'But I wanted to see the tracks close up, and continued moving towards them.

'The creature was definitely black - not the reddish brown mentioned in most Yeti sightings - and it followed me apparently monitoring my progress across the slope.

'But it remained equidistant with me, never getting any closer. This must have lasted another 15 minutes - then the creature disappeared behind the ridge. The snowstorm got worse and I did not see it again.

'I realise it is very possible to have subjective experiences at such high altitudes - but there was no mistaking these tracks.'

Impressions

The expedition had already monitored and checked out a whole series of tracks made by animals as varied as ibex and burrall, the wild mountain sheep. 'There is no question that these are very, very different indeed.

'Instead of light impressions on the snow, this animal had sunk in deeply, indicating that it was heavy as well as large.

'The creature I saw was very big indeed. It was a strange and frightening experience', said Davidson.

'And one I never want to repeat.'

Source: The Mail on Sunday 22/5/88

ASSIGNMENT ④

Read *Did I See the Yeti?* on page 71.

Imagine that you are John-Paul Davidson and that you are writing a diary account of your encounter with the creature known as a Yeti. Explain fully what happened and your feelings at the time. Look at the photo that follows. This creature is one that could be something like the Yeti we are talking about.

© *Rene Dahinden 1968. This Picture was taken from a distance of 24 metres*

ASSIGNMENT ⑤

As a group you wish to lead an expedition to find the Yeti. Imagine that you wish to gain sponsorship for such a venture.

Plan an advertising campaign to promote your venture and encourage people to sponsor you.

Design and write a leaflet that you could send out to firms explaining your intentions. The leaflet will need to contain detailed information about the Yeti and proof of its existence. You will also need to persuade companies to part with their money for a good reason. Remember that this leaflet must be eye-catching. The language you use is important. You must be convincing and persuasive.

ASSIGNMENT ⑥

Prepare a talk to accompany the leaflet that you have produced. Elect one person in the group to explain the venture you propose justifying the amount of money you need and why you think the firm should back you. This could include a detailed imaginative/informative map of the intended route and so on.

- How might you encourage a firm to sponsor you?
- What is in it for them?
- Try to plan the expedition as carefully as possible. Your venture must sound plausible.

ASSIGNMENT ⑦

Imagine you are a local business man and that you have to write a letter of reply to the above group of people who have sent you their leaflet. Explain fully why you would/would not be prepared to sponsor them. You must reply using letter layout. The content of the letter should depend heavily on whether you believe in the existence of a Yeti or not. You may wish to congratulate them or commiserate with them on the standard of their campaign!

ASSIGNMENT 8

Read the following extract taken from a poem by Margaret Atwood. It deals with the search for a Sasquatch and the discussion as to what will happen when it is found. The search is being conducted by a man and two androids.

The man disappears into the bush, and the two androids continue their learned discussion of the Sasquatch's importance to knowledge

ANDROID 1: *(rapidly) (in almost a prose voice)*
My aim is knowledge,
to know a thing I must probe it.

First I will capture it
with nets traps helicopters dogs pieces
of string holes dug in the ground doped food
tranquilizer guns buckshot thrown stones
bows and arrows

Then I will name the species
after myself

Then I will examine it
with pins tweezers flashlights microscopes
telescopes
envelopes statistics elastics
scalpels scissors razors lasers cleavers axes
rotary saws incisors osterizers pulverizers and
fertilizers.

I will publish the results
in learned journals

Then I will place a specimen
in each of the principle zoos
and a stuffed skin
in each of the principle museums
of the western world

When the breed nears extinction due to
hunters trappers loggers miners farmers
directors collectors inspectors

I will set aside a preserve consisting of:
   1 mountain
     1 lake
       1 river
         1 tree
           1 flower
             1 rock
               and 1 tall electric fence

ANDROID 2:
The things I want from it are:
   · 1 power
      2 fame
        3 money

I will get these things
pardon me,
achieve these goals by:

1 shooting it, thus proving it can be killed
   but only by one with skill and courage
   such as myself

2 posing for a front-page picture and/or a
   TV documentary with my boot on its neck
   and
   one hand casually on my hip

3 exhibiting, for a fee, the remains
   which have been preserved by:
     a stuffing
     b formaldehyde
     c freezing in ice

I will then make replicas from
~ fur coats
~ leather gloves
~ putty
~ inner tubes
~ piano keys
~ modelling clay
~ human hair

I will open a nationwide chain of man-monsters
I will retire at forty
and go fishing

The forest suddenly begins to stir, the androids hear strange sounds. Is it a Sasquatch? The androids fire their guns.

MARGARET ATWOOD

Look at the poem and then discuss the answers to the questions that follow. The questions will lead you through the poetry extract.

1 What does Android 1 want from finding the creature?

2 What will he do to the creature when he finds it?

3 What do you think of this?

4 What does the android predict will happen to the species? Why?

5 Does this bear any resemblance to what has happened to species before?

6 What do you think of that? Is it happening now? If so where?

7 What does Android 2 want from the creature?

8 Why does he amend the sentence 'I will get these things to . . . pardon me, achieve these goals by . . .'

9 Look at point 1. Why does the android add 'but only by one with skill and courage such as myself'?

10 What image is presented by point 2?

11 Do we make replicas of animals?

12 Can you imagine someone making a fortune in this way out of finding such a creature?

13 How do you feel about this poem? Has it made you think about the way we treat animals? Was this the intention of the poet perhaps?

 ASSIGNMENT

Imagine that a Yeti/Sasquatch/Big Foot has been captured. It is likely that more will be found and that the Yeti will be exploited like other species before it. Launch a campaign to 'Save the Yeti'.

1 Write a letter to your local MP condemning your local safari park's attempts to purchase a captured Yeti for display there.

2 Script a radio programme on which various people, scientists, anthropologists, explorers like Chris Bonington and animal rights groups discuss what should be done with or for this new species.

3 Devise a leaflet for nationwide distribution that is intended to persuade people to leave the Yeti alone.

- Remember what you have discussed.
- Use other species' history to back up your argument.
- Make it clear what you are doing and why.

INFORMATION WAS OBTAINED FROM:

- The Daily Telegraph Information Services.
- Dr Iain Bishop, The Natural History Museum. London.
- Mr David Heppell, The National Museum of Scotland. Edinburgh.
- *Manlike Monsters on Trial,* ed Marjorie Halpin and Michael Ames. Univ of British Columbia Press.

CHAPTER 8

ANGLING
THE NEGLECTED
BLOODSPORT

THE HUNTER | **THE HUNTED**

These scenes are typical of those to be found throughout the UK. The Campaign for the Abolition of Angling (CAA) needs your help in its fight to stop millions of anglers inflicting pain on fish, waterfowl and other creatures suffering as a direct result of this 'sport'.

Source: Campaign for the Abolition of Angling

ASSIGNMENT ①

Look at the posters and articles opposite and below.

1 Find out how many of the class have been fishing. (Over three and a half million people in this country fish.) What reasons do you or your classmates have for fishing? Is it enjoyable? Does it keep young people off the streets and out of mischief as the article claims?

2 Why should the numbers of people who take part in a sport be important?

3 Did you know that some political parties would like to abolish *all* field sports?
What does the class think of this?

4 Are there some sports you would abolish? Is fishing one of them? Why? It will be interesting to see if your views change either way as you read the following material.

5 Do you believe fish feel pain?

6 Why is fishing called a bloodsport on one poster and not a field sport?

7 What harm is done by fishermen to the environment according to the other poster?

WHY TAKE CHILDREN FISHING?

Last year the Angling Foundation sent out posters and information on fishing to some 9,000 schools.
The response was overwhelmingly enthusiastic, sales of typical beginners' rods have boomed, and many young people are now enjoying their second season in a new found sport.
Many of the benefits are endorsed by the comments from schools who took the initiative last year. But there are other important reasons for introducing pupils to angling.
Research has shown that youngsters who take up fishing and stay with it keep out of trouble; they have fun while they learn; they begin to appreciate the countryside, and to understand the environment. Above all, they enjoy a breath of fresh air in an outdoor, out of school activity that has to be preferable to lounging in front of the T .V .

HOW MANY ANGLERS ARE THERE?

Of the three and a half million who fish - the vast majority are ordinary working people!
The idea that people who hunt, shoot and fish do so because they are motivated by bloodlust is as illogical as the suggestion that people who enjoy lamb chops hate sheep!

Source: British Field Sports Society for the Campaign for Country Sports.

ALL THINGS BRIGHT AND BEAUTIFUL; ALL CREATURES GREAT AND SMALL

During the Vedanata conference on Animal Liberation held in Bath in August 1980, Svami Avyaktamanda, a dedicated devotee of 'Ahimsa' or non-violence, brought attention to the suffering of fish.

Our conscience has been suppressed completely as far as fishes are concerned. They are mercilessly taken from their natural environment, heaped up and subjected to slow death by the pressure of the heaps, gasping for breath.
Millions are caught everyday and are more ruthlessly treated than animals in experimentation, whose numbers are fewer.
Angling is unworthy of man. An innocent creature with a similar love of life to ours, is tempted onto a hook and compelled to bear the pain. When it is removed by force from the water, it is brought to a foreign environment where it cannot breathe, and suffers a slow death.

ishy

ASSIGNMENT ②

Read *Angling In Touch With Nature* and *Anglers and Conservation*. They were produced by people in favour of fishing. Look carefully at the information given you. Write a page and a half explaining what the poster and article are about and how they try to persuade you to adopt their point of view.

- Study the poster.
- Why is there a small boy in it?
- What is the reason for the caption on his tackle box?
- Have you ever seen all this wildlife around a stream, lake or river? Why is it shown here?
- Is this a realistic picture?
- Why is there a key?
- Why is it headed *Angling in Touch with Nature?*
- How does the article complement the poster?
- What have you learnt from the poster and the article?
- Does the language influence you at all? If so how does it do this?

ANGLERS AND CONSERVATION

There are many bodies actively involved in the conservation of our countryside and its wildlife. Anglers may not come to mind as leading exponents of nature conservation, but in fact they play a major, if unsung role in conserving wildlife.

The meaning of the term 'conservation' is sometimes misunderstood. It does not simply entail creating wildlife parks and nature reserves to protect rare or endangered species; neither does it involve the equivalent of wrapping the countryside in cling-film to protect it from outside influences. Effective conservation requires the sensibly directed management of fauna and flora and the environment in which they live.

In the case of shallow lakes, for example, this might take the form of careful dredging to remove silt, or of controlling encroaching reeds which would otherwise blanket the lake. Once restored, the water would provide much more suitable conditions for its wildlife than a similar, unmanaged lake, heading for sterility. Similarly, disused gravel pits used for angling are often fertilised by anglers to improve their biological productivity - the margins then being planted with trees and shrubs to make them still more productive as fisheries and more attractive in every way, offering fresh habitat to birds, small mammals and visually pleasing insects such as colourful butterflies.

The majority of still and running waters in Britain are controlled by anglers; many clubs and associations lease these fisheries from riparian owners; increasingly too, other angling groups have purchased such fisheries and the adjoining land, thereafter undertaking management exercises to preserve and improve the improve the fishing which their members demand.

Source: National Federation of Anglers

ANGLING
IN TOUCH WITH NATURE

KEY

1 Blue Tit	6 Heron
2 Long Tailed Tit	7 Kingfisher
3 Grey Squirrel	8 Mallard Duck
4 Brimstone Butterfly	9 Great Crested Grebe
5 Flat Bodied Dragonfly	10 Tufted Duck

KEY

11 Mute Swan	16 Bindweed
12 Common Carp	17 White Water Lily
13 Tench	18 Willow
14 Moorhen	19 Norfolk Reed
15 Dog Rose	20 Yellow Flag

ISSUED BY

NORFOLK ANGLERS CONSERVATION ASSOCIATION

ASSIGNMENT ③

You wish to start a fishing club in school. Design a poster to advertise this venture. As there is a rather strong anti-fishing group in school you will need to stress the advantages of fishing for young people.

You must persuade people to join your club and also persuade them that fishing is a worthwhile hobby.

ASSIGNMENT ④

Read the following pieces carefully.

Source: Pisces

WATERWAY USERS CONDEMN ANGLERS

In December last year, *"Waterways World"*, a magazine for boaters and waterways enthusiasts, published a CAA letter requesting details of angling aggravation experienced by its readers.

The response was amazing. Many correspondents highlighted the fact that anglers seem to think they have a greater right to use waterways. Another common cause for complaint is anglers' inconsiderate and anti-social behaviour. Finally, many correspondents mentioned the deaths of fish and birds at the hands of anglers.

"I live canalside and anglers are a constant source of irritation. About a year ago I arrived home from a short towpath walk with my dogs to find one of them had got her legs tangled in several feet of fishing line with lead weights and she had a fish hook stuck through her neck. About an hour of struggling to detach the hook resulted in a visit to our local vet to have it removed. He says he frequently has similar cases to deal with.

One fellow recently had his umbrella rope anchored not only across the towpath but into the hedge making it impossible to get by. I unhooked it and pointed out that the path was for walking on and not just for his use. He instantly pegged it back into the hedge and on my return I unpegged it again, asking for his name. Needless to say I received a mouthful.

The towpath is littered, particularly after a match, by plastic bags, tackle, lunch wrappers, discarded bread, bait and maggots. Drink bottles and cans are thrown into my garden. I have several times had the displeasure of seeing them relieve themselves in the hedge at the front of my home - one I caught urinating into my flowerbed ....

Apart from all this, we find fish that have died, presumably from stress as much as anything, after these competitions, being a canal, they simply float back and forth past the house for days, gradually decomposing. A disturbing sight."

"......I would describe anglers as stupid, arrogant, obstructive and selfish. I would be very happy to see them abolished completely from our canals and rivers."

".....The bank opposite was regularly used by fishermen who would have contests on most weekends...... Any thoughts we may have had about a Sunday morning lie-in were shattered as they shout to one another along the towpath as they set up about 6.30am. After they had finished and the catch had been bounced around on the scales net before being hurled back into the water, we would see fish dead and dying on the surface.

During one winter I saw something hanging from a tree in our garden.... On closer inspection I found that this was the remains of a starling which had swallowed a length of fishing line and become entangled in the tree..... this summer I noticed a young, dead moorhen hanging by one foot from a length of line about five feet up in the branches of a hedge at the side of the canal..... Lined up on the opposite bank was - you've guessed it - a dozen fishermen."

Source: Pisces April/June '88

Source: National Federation of Anglers

ANGLERS RAISE £15,000 FOR CANCER RESEARCH

ON SATURDAY 3rd October, NFA members joined with our NASA colleagues in a sponsored fish-in in aid of Cancer Research.

The event took place at Weir Wood near East Grinstead in Sussex and more than 300 anglers from different parts of the country took part.

Although a number of the competitors took the fishing seriously, for the majority it was seen as a fun day with the prime objective to attain the £10,000 target set for the fish-in.

Although at the time of writing all of the money had not yet been received, it appears that the target will be exceeded and it is now expected more than £15,000 will be raised for Cancer Research by the event. A number of individual competitors are believed to have raised almost £1,000 each.

Source: Course Angler Magazine

PETER COCKWILL
Talking Trout

GET IT OVER QUICKLY

HOW do you kill your first fish? Does it die quickly with one neat blow or does it need repeat bashings until it resembles pate rather than a trout!

There is only one method and that is to dispose of the fish as quickly and humanely as possible.

Don't be frightened of the job and follow a few basic tips.

Number one is to have a decent weight of priest. Mine weighs in at 12oz and nothing argues after getting a bash with that. One that only weighs an ounce or so will be OK for tiny fish but with anything of size it's going to take a lot of hits and then the whole job becomes a bit messy.

Secondly, you should keep the fish in the meshes of the net, that way you can get a good grip on its slippery body and won't risk having it wriggle about so that it gets hit in the wrong spot or, worse still, you hit your own finger.

Boy does that hurt! Third is to make sure that the fish is hit in the right spot. Hold it upright in the net meshes with its belly on the ground and your left hand over the top of it and just in front of the dorsal fin.

Now give it one good hard blow at the junction of head and body. There may be a momentary quiver afterwards but that's it, all over.

Source: Anglers Mail 19/3/88

FISH FARMER FINED

DEAD terns hanging over a fish farm alerted birdwatchers in Dorset who contacted the RSPB. The fish farmer, Peter Pratt, told investigators that he had asked an employee to shoot gulls flying over the pools. Two common and two black terns were shot and hung up - a practice widely used by gamekeepers.

Black terns are rare passage migrants and are given special protection under the Wildlife and Countryside Act. Mr Pratt was fined £300 in respect of the dead black terns and £100 for the common terns.

Source: Pisces

HOW ANGLERS PROTECT THE ENVIRONMENT

To pursue their sport anglers need clean water. Although other water based sports might prefer cleaner water, they have no special incentive to strive to achieve it. In contrast, the very essence of angling is that it demands conditions capable of supporting animal and plant life.

Britain's Industrial Revolution left many of our waterways at the mercy of the polluters whose cheap and simple recourse was to pour their industrial waste into the nearest river - a disaster for Britain's watercourses and their associated wildlife. Excellent fisheries in the late 1800s became stinking, rubbish-filled open sewers by the turn of the century. Laws passed in 1876 were intended to give local authorities the power to prosecute polluters, but they themselves were often the biggest culprits. In the first half of the next century, the situation became even worse.

It was against this apparently hopeless background that John Eastwood saw the possibility of using the Common Law against polluters. In 1948 the Anglers' Co-operative Association (ACA) was formed to tackle pollution in this way, and within months of its formation it had begun to score successes.

In 1951 it fought its most renowned case, on behalf of two Derby angling clubs, against British Celanese, Derby Corporation and East Midlands Tar Distillers. These bodies had between them been responsible for releasing millions of gallons of untreated sewage and tar products into the Derbyshire Derwent, causing pollution which destroyed the river as a life support system and part of the River Trent into which it flowed. The ACA won the case, with costs and damages awarded against the defendants. Even today, a court injunction bars the offenders in question from repeating their pollutive action.

In 1953, a serious polluter of the Welsh Dee was successfully prosecuted by the ACA. In 1954 the Consett Iron Company alleged that the ACA had no right to take legal action to prevent pollution from their works, but failed. That was a landmark.

Since then the ACA has continued to employ the law against polluters. Throughout its 40 years of existence, it has lost only one case, due to a technical change in the law while the case was pending. Such is its reputation now that most of the cases the ACA takes up on behalf of anglers are settled out of court, with adequate compensation being paid to the plaintiff.
The nature of pollution is changing, though - untreated industrial wastes have been replaced by agricultural pollution, from silage clamps, flooded slurry lagoons and - ironically - from trout farms sited on our most prestigious trout rivers. The faeces from millions of trout can cause acute pollution downstream of the farm's outfall.

In 1986, the ACA brought a common law prosecution against a trout farm on the West Beck, in North Humberside - action which would have been impossible under the statutory law. In April 1987, the ACA went further, taking the historic step of prosecuting Thames Water Authority for that body's failure to meet its own discharge consents on Aylesbury sewage works, which was polluting the River Thame.

The ACA, in short, is the only water-based, voluntary anti-pollution body in Britain, and among the ranks of conservationists, it can claim a unique record.

Forty years after the formation of the ACA, anglers are still as vigilant as ever. To the angler his recreational environment is a complete 'package.' It starts with the clean water he must have for fish to survive, and it is complimented by the bankside life which his efforts support: the kingfisher darting along the river and the bank vole which swims in the margins. They are as much part of the angler's world as the dimpling dace or the leaping salmon.

Anglers are the eyes and ears of the waterside and keep a continuous watch on the aquatic environment.

Date: September 1988

Source: National Federation of Anglers

ASSIGNMENT ⑤

Make a list of all the reasons that anglers would use to defend their sport. You will need to look at *all* the information you have been given. Then make another list that outlines all the reasons why animal rights campaigners would be against fishing.

ASSIGNMENT ⑥

Read *How Anglers Protect the Environment*.

Design a leaflet which explains why the Anglers' Co-operative was formed and which encourages young fishermen/women from your school to join. This should be suitable for printing on one page only and for being sent out to school children from age 11 onwards, who have just joined school fishing clubs. You will need to be prepared for questions.

ASSIGNMENT ⑦

You live alongside a canal and have been asked to speak at a public meeting arranged by the householders. The meeting is to discuss the litter, nuisance and environmental damage that is being caused by local fishermen. Local anglers have been invited to state their case.

Plan this work well, deciding in advance who is to play the householders and who the anglers. Remember to use all the information about fishing that you have read. You will need to be prepared for questions.

ASSIGNMENT ⑧

Your local MP has put forward a motion in parliament asking for the banning of all field sports and in particular fishing. Write a letter to her/him explaining with reasons your feelings on this issue. Your letter should either support your MP or oppose the motion put forward.

INFORMATION WAS OBTAINED FROM:

- The Campaign for the Abolition of Fishing. P.O. Box 14, Romsey SO14 9NN
- The Angling Foundation. P.O. Box 156 Croydon CR9 3TD
- British Field Sports Society. 59 Kennington Road, London SE1 7PZ.
- National Anglers Council. 11 Cowgate, Peterborough PE1 1LZ
- National Federation of Anglers. Halliday House. 2 Wilson Street, Derby DE1 1PG.

fishing

CHAPTER 9

Many animals are hunted for their fur – seals, otters, wolves, coyotes, lynx, foxes, raccoons, badgers, colobus monkeys and so on. The list is an extensive one. Some animals which are valued for their fur are also bred in captivity on factory farms.

ASSIGNMENT

Read the poem, *Colobus Monkey.*

Look at the following questions and discuss them.

1 What is the poem about?

2 Look at the picture of the colobus. Why do you think its fur is so prized?

3 Would you be interested in a coat that was made of this? Give reasons for your answer.

4 How many people in your group have a fur coat?

5 What do you think is meant by the phrase 'cheeks full of laughter'?

6 What is the purpose of the second verse?

7 Why is a housewife mentioned?

8 What has the housewife got in common with the eagle and the colobus?

9 Why is the colobus too beautiful to live?

10 Why is it unlikely to survive?

11 What do you think of the poem and how does it fit in with the theme of the chapter?

Now write your own account of the poem explaining how you felt about its theme.

COLOBUS MONKEY

We invite him to die
he smiles
He dies at last
his cheeks full of laughter
Two rows of bared white teeth.

At daybreak
the housewife sweeps the floor
the eagle sweeps the sky
and colobus
sweeps the top of his tree.

Abuse him
and he will follow you home
Praise him
and he leaves you alone.
The ragged man
and the man in the embroidered gown
both covet his skin.

Lice killer
with black nails
deep-set eyes
sweeping tail
Too beautiful to live.
Death always follows greed.
Too beautiful to survive
death always follows war.

FROM THE YORUBA *(trans Ulli Beier)*

ASSIGNMENT ②

Read the poem again and *Witness to a Killing*. Write
a page explaining how you feel about the fur trade
after reading these two pieces.
Note: *a full length coyote skin coat can be bought
at a London furrier for betwen £4,500 and £7,000.*

WITNESS TO A KILLING

A CHILLING ACCOUNT OF HOW A TRAPPED COYOTE WAS KILLED FOR ITS FUR

Bullets are not used to kill trapped animals because they damage fur. The two most common methods of killing furbearers are repeated bludgeoning of the head, and a practice called "suffocation", when the trapper stands on the animal's vital organs — usually for 14 to 15 minutes — until life leaves the body. This method is shown as photographed by wildlife researcher Daniel Kelly at Turnbull National Wildlife Refuge, Washington. (U.S. Congressional Testimony, 1976). Kelly's account of how a trapper kills his prey:

"Both front legs caught in traps, the coyote, exhausted after four days of fighting the unyielding steel, crouched against the tree stump, his piercing yellow eyes still alertly focused on my every movement. Thoughts of mercifully killing or releasing the animal were fleeting as an approaching car brought a rush of reality. A man in his 60s emerged from the car expressing surprise and resentment at my presence. Once an understanding had been established, the trapper set about the business of disposing of the trapped coyote. The trapper approached, a five-foot green birch club in hand. The coyote struggled frantically against the traps, pulling one leg loose and leaving the

lifeless paw in the trap. The trapper poked at the coyote. The animal hissed and snapped at the club. Then, as the trapper slowly swished the club back and forth, the coyote became unusually calm. Mesmerized by the steady motion, he crouched motionless, his yellow eyes dutifully following the swishing club.

Suddenly the club smashed across the coyote's nose and slammed him to the ground. But the blow was not delivered with precision. Almost instantly he was

LAST YEAR MORE THAN 300,000 COYOTES WERE AMONGST THE 20 MILLION WILD ANIMALS TRAPPED AND KILLED FOR THEIR FUR

THE
LYNX
EDUCATIONAL TRUST
FOR
ANIMAL
WELFARE

PO Box 509, Dunmow, Essex CM6 1UH

in a semi-crouch; blood spurting from the nose, eyes dazed, Again the club fell. The trapper, in one practiced motion, grabbed the stunned coyote by the hind legs, stretching the animal full length while planting his foot heavily on its neck. The other foot delivered a series of thumping blows to the coyote's chest expelling hollow gasps of air. Releasing the hind legs, the trapper rested one foot on the coyote's neck, the other on the chest. The coyote's eyes bulged, the mouth gaped, the tongue hung listlessly along the blood-stained jaw. Periodically stomping near the heart, the trapper maintained this position for 14 minutes. He indicated this was necessary to ensure that the animal was dead — 'Once had one leap up and take a bite at me.' There was no emotion involved, only a degree of disgust when the blow fell short or a brief expression of satisfaction when the blow was effective; the coyote was a varmint and was treated as such. While focussing the camera, I thought now ridiculous it was for a 200-pound man to be stomping on an 18-pound coyote as if his very existence depended on the animal's elimination. The coyote, had he been given the opportunity, would not even have sought revenge. He would only have tried to escape.

Satisfied the coyote was dead, the trapper added several final stomps before releasing the remaining trap. Reluctantly, I accepted his offer to accompany him down the road. The carcass was dumped into the trunk along with the wide-eyed carcass of another. Thirty more sets yielded another coyote, a badger, a raccoon and two magpies. These coyotes were trapped under the auspices of 'recreational trapping'."

ASSIGNMENT ③

Many people rely on fur trading for their livelihood. Read the extract *Destruction of Seal Market Fuels Inuit Suicides*. Make a list of the points made in this article that could be used by people defending their need to hunt.

ASSIGNMENT ④

Write a letter from Jaypoatie to the Government highlighting the problems faced by Innuit people and offering solutions that they could implement to help ease the situation and halt the number of suicides among young people.

DESTRUCTION OF SEAL MARKET FUELS INUIT SUICIDES

By MATTHEW FISHER

The Globe and Mail, Broughton Island

When Jaypoatie and his friend Saulu stroll along the frozen shore of Baffin Bay, their conversation is not carefree teenage chit chat. Like everyone in Broughton Island, the 15 year old Inuit are haunted by a growing teenage suicide epidemic and a future of welfare cheques and satellite television images depicting a vibrant, distant society of which they will never be part.

During the past two years, about one-third of the hamlet's 60 teenagers between the ages of 15 and 18 have attempted suicide. Eight have succeeded, including Jaypoatie's 16 year old sister. "She tried it a lot of times but my mother always caught her until she finally hung herself last January in Clyde River," Jaypoatie said in the matter-of-fact monotone of the Inuit.

When asked why his sister felt she must end her life, the small Grade 8 student shrugged, "I don't know why she did it," he said, finally. "I guess she was bored." Since animal-rights activists in the South and in Europe succeeded in destroying the traditional seal harvest in the early 1980's, the local economy in this area 2,600 kilometres north of Montreal has been paralyzed. With European markets closed, the price of seal pelts plummeted from $32 to $5 or $6.

Broughton Island hunters used to produce the highest per capita seal harvest in North America - 11,000 pelts a year - but now harvest fewer than 1,000. This has resulted in a 95 per cent unemployment rate and increasingly pervasive ennui. If a young man or woman is unable to secure one of 17 jobs offered by the hamlet, there is little to do except play sports in the local gymnasium, watch television or listen to music. "The teenagers tell us there are no jobs and there is no place to go," said the island's mayor, Keesak Audlakiak. "If the Bay was buying seal the young kids could go out hunting. Instead they listen to rock music.

"I was a lot happier when I was a teenager because I could go out hunting all day. Suicide was something that almost never happened. Mar

Audlakiak explained that a two day trip by snowmobile to teach his children to hunt for seals costs about $100 in fuel. "And when we hunt we get nothing back for it, so we often don't go. Inuit don't hunt unless there is a reason."

Broughton Island is one of the few Eastern Arctic communities without a full time Anglican priest. The nearest clergyman is Benjamin Arreak, 200 kilometres to the south, in Pangnirtung, and he can visit only infrequently.

"Only the old people used to commit suicide in the Inuit culture, and that was only if they became a burden to their families as they moved around hunting animals," Mr Arreak said. "Perhaps the main reason the young are doing it is because of the confusion they are experiencing because of our changing culture. Answers are given by pressing a button, but you cannot solve life's problems by pressing buttons. Suicide is a way to escape this for those who see no purpose in living."

Mr Arreak said that from his many talks with Inuit youth he suspected drugs and rock music had a lot to do with their feelings of inadequacy and futility. With drugs and heavy rock, they tell me, they communicate with spirits which urge them to commit suicide," the pastor said. "This is very new to me, It's only in the past four years I have heard such things." Mr Audlakiak has listened to the same bizarre stories. "Teenagers have told me that the devil talks to them through rock music, telling them to die, to hang themselves."

The chief executive officer of the Baffin Regional Health Board, Trevor Porritt, said: "When you wake up in the winter and it's dark and cold and there is no work, what incentive is there to get out of bed? There isn't even any privacy because most of the homes are badly overcrowded. So, if you're honest you'll admit there is nothing to get up for. Without the seal industry, these communities have nothing."

With the birth rate among the Inuit challenging that of Third World countries such as Kenya and no prospects for a viable sealing industry, the employment crisis will soon become much worse. Mr Porritt said:

"The only solution is dramatic government intervention to undo the effects of the sealing boycott by creating heavily subsidized businesses, he said. The new Government Leader of the NWT, Dennis Patterson said: "A third of our population is under the age of 14, so we're facing frightening social problems. Drug and alcohol abuse and the suicide epidemic are evidence of a profound malaise. "Our only hope is to provide those kids with something to do. We somehow have to break the cycle of economic dependency of government through economic development. To control our own future we must acquire more control over our natural resources."

More than 100 of Broughton Islands's 400 residents recently attended a meeting at which the hamlet council, the Housing Association, the Hunters and Trappers Association, the Anglican church, and federal and territorial agencies discussed ways to halt the succession of suicide attempts. As a result of the unprecedented gathering, four young adults have been appointed as youth counsellors. One of them, Anthony Itsanilk, a 27 year old "odd job man" has lost cousins and a niece in the suicide epidemic. When he was a teenager he tried to commit suicide several times. "I'm not happy to say it, but there is going to be more suicide," Mr Itsanilk said. "When there is nothing to do and no place to go, it seems like a good idea sometimes. What I am going to try and tell them is to think more about the future and ways they can do things that give life meaning."

Broughton Island's maintenance foreman Elwood Johnston, said he and a few other adults have started a boxing club for teenagers. He is also establishing an apprentice mechanic program and hopes to arrange an apprentice electrician program. "It really shakes me up to see what is happening here because this is a good town, a really good town."

Source: The Globe Mail 29/12/87

ASSIGNMENT ⑤

Read *The Fascinating World of Fur, Fur and the Fury* and *Help Us Get the Fur Trade Off the Nation's Back* (page 91).

If the fur trade were abolished tomorrow, make a list explaining who would benefit and who would suffer. You need to think about animals and humans for this.

As the larger cat species became scarce and protected, so the fur trade turned its attention to the smaller cats such as the ocelot, margay, lynx and the little known Geoffroy's cat. These smaller cat species are now being trapped and hunted in large numbers. In 1982, no fewer than 28,000 lynx were trapped for the fur trade in Canada alone. In 1984, to give another alarming example of wild life destruction, more than 13,000 skins of Geoffroy's cat were imported into France from Bolivia, while West Germany imported 16,980 leopard cat skins from China. Wild animal populations cannot withstand such heavy losses and LYNX campaigns for their total protection in the wild.

- How would the factory farmers be affected?
- Think about the chain of which they are the first link.
- How would the trapper be affected?
- What effect would it have on the environment?
- How would animal rights groups be affected?
- How would people in the average British street be affected?
- How would people who live in very cold climates be affected?

THE FASCINATING WORLD OF FUR...

Where fur comes from

85 per cent of furs used the world over come from animals which are ranched and farmed. Government schemes to keep wild animal population levels healthy provide most of the rest. The British fur trade was an early advocate of protection of endangered species and a law was passed in 1976 to forbid their importation. Furs come to London from all over the world to be auctioned to international buyers.

Fur in history

Fur was one of the earliest forms of clothing. The animals Man hunted for their meat also provided him with warm covering. In the Middle Ages fur was a symbol of power and ermine the emblem of kingship.

Explorers made long and dangerous voyages to find new supplies. North America was opened up by traders looking for furs. Throughout history men have worn as much fur as women — a fashion which is now reviving.

The two main species of ranched furs are mink and fox but there are many species of wild fox and other types of foxes and mink.

Making a fur coat

After being auctioned skins are subjected to improve the suppleness of the leather and the softness of the fur. Some are used in the natural colour, others are dyed and bleached. Skins are then sorted by size, colour and quality, and piles are matched (come punched)...

Sometimes skins are let out. This is America. That is a delicate cutting and sewing operation which makes the skin longer but narrower before the pattern is cut and with precision finds elegant lines.

The cut and design of a fur coat are all important. A new design is first made up in cloth, to ensure that everything is correct before the pattern is cut...

Next the cutter carefully matches the prepared skins and cuts the various parts of the coat (sleeves, collars) to the pattern.

When the skins have been sewn together the parts are damped and tacked down to a board on which the pattern has been traced.

When the skins dry they retain the outline or curved lines of the coat pattern shapes. They are then re-formed from the board.

First region picking type precision stretching and the work is most often finished by hand. The actual sewing of skins is done by specially designed, motorised sewing machines which needs care, and practice and much patience special skill.

CAREERS IN THE FUR TRADE

A lot of delicate and intricate work goes into the making of a fur coat. If you choose to work in this trade you can see the results of your craftsmanship in each individual garment. The basic requirements for a boy or girl learning a craft are: good eye-sight (with or without glasses), a steady hand and a sound general education. If you enjoy detailed work which needs care and patience, you could enjoy one of these skilled jobs.

Most firms are small and can offer each new entrant the chance to work in several departments to find out which is the most suitable job. Almost all training is done in the company, but there are opportunities to attend short courses organised by groups of companies or by an auction house.

'Learning the trade' beginning with one of these crafts, may be the first step towards a job in which you supervise the work of others or take responsibility for buying, selling or design.

Many of today's firms were started off by people who entered the trade as school-leavers. You could become your own boss too.

WANT MORE INFORMATION ?

Further information on the industry is available from

The British Fur Trade Association
68 Upper Thames Street, London EC4V 3AN

Clothing and Allied Products Industry Training Board
Tower House, Merrion Way, Leeds LS2 8NY

Source: The British Fur Trade Association

ASSIGNMENT 6

Look at the article *Fur and the Fury* and then look at the LYNX poster *Help Us To Get the Fur Trade Off the Nation's Back* on page 88. Compare the way both organisations present their material. How effective do you think each style of presentation is likely to be?

- What is the article *Fur and the Fury* about?
- Is the language used informative or emotive?
- What does the information presented by LYNX look like? Does it differ a lot from the RSPCA article? If so, what reasons can you suggest for this?
- Which material is the most informative?
- Which is the most effective?
- What are the purposes of the organisations?
- Are they different? Could this affect the approach?

ASSIGNMENT 7

Write two paragraphs explaining the difference between factory farming of fur and fur trapping.

ASSIGNMENT 8

Read the article *Fur and the Fury* again. Plan two radio commercials. One is produced by LYNX and draws public attention to the damage that is done by the fur trade. The second is commissioned by *The Fur Traders Association* and is encouraging young people to join the industry.

ASSIGNMENT 9

Discuss the arguments that a person who wishes to have a fur coat could make in their defence. Should someone have to defend their right to own something?

- How would you feel if someone told you that you couldn't do something or have something?
- Does this happen to you at all?
- When and why?
- How does the fur trade aid employment?
- Who would lose out if no fur coats were made?
- Is this a valid argument?
- Is there any difference, for you, between fur taken from animals killed in the wild and fur taken from animals bred specifically for the purpose?
- How far should people be allowed to go in trying to impose their wishes on others? Do you agree that some illegal behaviour is justified?
- Is a dangerous precedent set when people try to justify illegal behaviour for certain reasons?

FUR AND THE FURY

By Stefan Ormrod
RSPCA Chief Wildlife Officer

Opposition to the fur trade has almost solely been engendered by concern for the species of animal involved, not concern for the individual animal. The Sea Otter, *Enhydra lutris,* provides a typical example. Its skin was one of the most sought after pelts in the fur trade and in 1856 the Russian-American Company sold 118,000 Sea otter skins. So great was the hunting pressure on this species, that by 1885 only 8,000 pelts were traded and by 1910 the number had diminished to 400. The high prices paid for this creature's fur, and the resultant intensive pursuit almost led to the animal's extinction, but fortunately a few survived and thanks to protective legislation, the Sea otter population has gradually increased.

Many animals have suffered a similar fate at the hands of the fur trade. Seals immediately spring to mind. The actual killing of seals has nothing whatsoever in common with population control or fisheries protection, it is a barbaric harvest which has frequently resulted in indiscriminate persecution. Several species of fur seals have been dramatically reduced by this hunting pressure. Those found in Guadalupe Island off Lower California, on the coasts and islands of South America, and South Africa, around the southern tip of New Zealand and on adjacent islands and on many sub-Antarctic islands of the southern Indies and Atlantic Oceans have all fared extremely badly at the hands of man.

The present world-wide outcry against the annual butchery of Harp seals has been a source of encouragement to welfarists and conservationalists alike, for it has resulted in a voluntary European ban on imports which should become a mandatory two year ban later this year. Public opinion has been successful before. The 'teddy-bear' of the Australian eucalyptus forests, the koala, was also a victim of the fur trade and by the mid 1920's over a million skins were exported. The species population declined rapidly but, due to pressure from the public, it was granted protection just in time and is now showing signs of recovery.

It has been the same story all over the world. Whenever an animal has been unfortunate enough to have soft luxurious or handsomely marked skin, it has been killed off mercilessly for the sake of human vanity. Endangered species legislation offers great hope for species that have been, or are now being, decimated by the fur trade. But is this enough? It should be remembered that some authorities and governments only assign animals to the endangered category when they are on the brink of extinction, while other authorities determine a species endangered as soon as its population becomes depleted and losses far exceed natural recruitment.

Some species are not endangered, or are not known to be, owing to insufficient biological research, and for these creatures there is not protection. Cruelty is rarely considered in international wildlife protection. Yet cruelty is, and always has been, a feature of the fur trade. Within the past ten years trapping has intensified greatly as fur markets have boomed and pelt prices have risen astronomically. The steel jaw leghold trap (banned in England and Wales since 1958 and Scotland since 1973) is the instrument of death for 80% of wild fur-bearing animals in the United States. It is a viciously cruel instrument that slams shut on the animal's paw, frequently shattering the bone, and the unfortunate creature may remain in the trap until it eventually starves to death. Prior to that merciful release it will suffer pain, trauma, hunger and thirst unless, as many do, it escapes by chewing off its own paw.

The suffering involved is incalculable. The 1977/78 total for wildlife killed in the USA alone was 18,784,261!

A SPECIAL MESSAGE

*T*he impact on the European boycott on sealskin products and large-scale campaigns against the trapping of fur bearing animals is destroying traditional aboriginal lifestyles and cultures that have existed in harmony with nature for thousands of years.

The impact is particularly being felt throughout Canada's Arctic Northwest Territories where Inuit, Inuvialuit, Dener and Metis people attempt to maintain a fine balance between traditional lifestyles and the modern wage economy in order to preserve their cultural identities and to care for their families.

It is on the land and on the water that we gain a sense of achievement and identity from our traditional pursuits of hunting, trapping and fishing.

Animals, fish and sea mammals we harvest are used as our primary source of nutrition and money from the sale of products manufactured from the skins and furs is used to supplement the precarious and fragile economy that exists in most northern settlements.

In recent years, however, the sealskin boycott and anti trapping lobbies have created marginal fur prices forcing many of us to abandon our traditional lifestyles.

What is not understood by many non-native Canadians, North Americans and Europeans is the nutritional, educational, social and total cultural dependence we have as aboriginal people on the use of what non-native people call wildlife resources. To us, these resources are our agricultural base - a base that we have harvested for thousands of years.

More importantly, we have adopted the scientific tools of animal husbandry developed in the 20th Century to ensure these valuable resources are there for our use, the use of our children and for future generations. Modern society's concern over environmental pollution, access to clean water, protection of animal, fish and sea mammals, and the wise use of the land are our concerns as well.

We have long recognized that these modern interpretations are necessary to protect these foundations and heritage of the Inuit, Inuvialuit, Dene and Metis cultures in the Northwest Territories. Our ancestors passed the same concepts on to us.

In conclusion, this material will hopefully help Canadian, North American and European audiences and government leaders to understand the aboriginal people's point of view.

We are anticipating that the consequences of prolonged boycotts of sea mammal products and the effects of the anti-fur lobby will be disastrous to the aboriginal peoples of the Canadian Northwest Territories.

We ask that you consider our side of the story in detail and that you question the value of supporting emotionally-based anti-sealing and anti-fur boycotts and lobbies in light of their effects on other cultures which depend upon the harvest of animal and sea resources for their way of life.

Jim Bovine Deputy Minister of Renewable Resources.

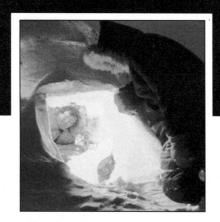

Source: Northwest Territories Renewable Sources.

ASSIGNMENT

Imagine that a well-known pop star was attacked recently in the press for repeatedly wearing fur garments. Yesterday the same star was attacked by an animal rights campaigner who threw red paint over a coat the star was wearing. The star was unhurt, the fur was ruined and the animal rights campaigner was arrested. Write a newspaper article that reports on the attack and also includes detailed interviews with both parties involved. You should aim to bring out their opinions on the issue. At the end of some newspaper articles newspaper reporters make clear whose side they are on. Try doing this in as strong a manner as possible.

ASSIGNMENT

Read *A special message* carefully.

Read the following assignment titles and then choose to write on one of them. Your work should be at least 300–400 words long.

1 'I am personally sick of all the do-gooders who tell me that I should not even want a fur coat. Because I find fur attractive and like wearing it, I am told that I am heartless and moreover vain. I am sick of these hypocrites who still wear leather shoes, wear wool jumpers and eat meat; yet tell me I shouldn't wear my mink coat. What is the difference between a mink farm, a chicken farm, a dairy farm? – You tell me because the difference escapes me.' Write about how you feel about this person's point of view.

2 'I am an Inuit Indian. Animal Rights campaigners are encouraging my government to reduce and reduce the hunting and trapping that is our way of life. Each reduction puts another nail in the coffin of my people. In time only the animals will remain – there will be no Inuit. Are we destined to become extinct also? Does no one care about Man's endangered races?' What do you think about the comments made by this Inuit Indian? Imagine that the animal rights campaigners, the Inuit and members of the government are taking part in a discussion in a hall in the Inuit community. Write in play form the discussion that might take place, with each party stating their case as they see it.

3 Imagine that you are a campaigner on behalf of one of the endangered species described in this chapter. Write an account of how you feel about the fur trade and the way it has affected your chosen species.

INFORMATION WAS OBTAINED FROM:

- Compassion in World Farming. 20 Lavant Street, Petersfield, Hants GU32 3EW
- LYNX. PO Box 509, Dunmow, Essex CM6 1UH.
- RSPCA. The Causeway, Horsham, Sussex RH12 1ZA.
- Animal Aid.
- The British Fur Trade Association. 68 Upper Thames Street, London EC4.
- Clothing and Allied Products Industry Training Board. Tower House, Merrion Way, Leeds LS2 8NY.

CHAPTER 10
Ghosts

ghosts: fantasy or fact

✝

ASSIGNMENT ❶

Read and discuss *Ghost Busters* and *So You Think You Know About Ghosts*. Do you believe in any of the types of ghost described here? Do you think it is possible to 'bust' a ghost? Write a page explaining your reactions.

ghost busters!

There's something new in your
neighbourhood
Who you going to call? Ghostbusters!
There's something weird and it don't look
good,
Who you going to call? Ghostbusters!
I ain't 'fraid of no ghost!
I ain't 'fraid of no ghost!

You seeing things running through your
head,
Who you going to call? Ghostbusters!
An invisible man sleeping in your bed,
Who you going to call? Ghostbusters!
I ain't 'fraid of no ghost!
I ain't 'fraid of no ghost!

Who you going to call? Ghostbusters!
If you're all alone pick up the phone
And call Ghostbusters.
I ain't 'fraid of no ghost,
I ain't 'fraid of no ghost,
I hear it likes gals
I ain't 'fraid of no ghost.
Yeh, Yeh, Yeh, Yeh.
Who you going to call? Ghostbusters!
If you're all alone pick up the phone and call
Ghostbusters!
Let me tell ya something,
Busting makes me feel good,
I ain't 'fraid of no ghost
Who you goin to call? Ghostbusters!
If you're all alone pick up the phone and call

Ghostbusters
Who you goin to call? Ghostbusters!
You've had a dose of a freaky ghost,
Baby, you'd better call Ghostbusters,
Don't get caught all alone, Oh, No! Ghostbusters,
When it comes through your door,
Unless you want some more - I think you'd better call
Ghostbusters! (Fade ....)

Words and Music by Ray Parker Junior

SO YOU THINK YOU KNOW ABOUT GHOSTS!

Haunting Ghosts ~ These are seen by many
different people and at different times. They are
attracted by the place which they haunt and always
appear in the same place and look the same.
Animals can be ghosts.

Ghosts of the Living ~ Some ghosts seen are
actually ghosts of living people. They are seen by
close relatives or friends. The person whose ghost it
is could be miles away at the time it is seen. Such
ghosts may only be seen once or twice.

Some ghosts appear only to carry out a purpose.
They are the ghosts of dead people who appear to
give a warning or messages to family or friends.
These ghosts might not speak.

Many legends tell of ghosts who have returned to
avenge a wrong and to expose a guilty villain.

They make sure that money or property is returned
to the rightful owner.

Ghosts may come back to right a wrong that they
have committed.

Sometimes ghosts reveal the hiding place in which
they hoarded money or treasure.

Poltergeists ~ They are supposedly responsible for
some alarming aspects of the supernatural, such as
cups and saucers flying through the air. Objects
being moved during poltergeist activity can behave
oddly. They may be too hot to handle. They move
through gaps, spaces normally too small to allow
them through. They can also appear in mid-air.

Poltergeist activity usually happens when young
people between the ages of 12-16 are present
although it is not known why. One theory supposes
that their minds may generate the mysterious power
needed. Researchers call this unknown power
Psychokinesis ~ PK ~ the ability to move objects
without touching them. If they are correct and **PK**
exists, then there are no ghosts involved, just the
side effects of **PK** energy.

ASSIGNMENT 2

Study the article *No, You Can't Walk Out on a Poltergeist*.
Imagine that you are Mrs Cotterill or a member of her family. You have to persuade the judge that the haunting is genuine. Write out the statement that you would give in court, basing your ideas on the material given.

COUNCIL FIGHT THE 'HAUNTED' FAMILY FROM NO 124

No, you can't walk out on a poltergeist

by James Golden

AS haunted houses go, number 124, Melbourne Road lacks a certain something. No gothic towers, no wild forest lashing the windows, and definitely no cadaverous butler.

Yet within this three-bedroom, council semi lurks a terror that drove a family to flee, telling tales of mysterious music and a guest who went bump in the night.

Yesterday, the curious case of the Nottingham poltergeists occupied the High Court as John and Helen Costello continued their battle with the city council which refuses to rehouse them.

A judge heard that the couple saw plugs pulled out of their sockets by invisible hands, heard their electric organ play mournful music by itself and the electric guitar strum, both without being plugged in.

Bedding was removed as they slept and a window shattered without apparent reason. When a priest splashed holy water on the stairs in hope of exorcising the spirits, the water was blown back in his face.

A retired legal executive who spent the night at the 1920s-built house in Aspley, Nottingham, was lifted bodily from the sofa by an unseen force.

Social workers and police also witnessed the strange happening, but the city council refused to rehouse the tormented family.

Misgivings

And when the couple moved out with their 13-year-old daughter, Rose, councillors decided they did not deserve another house because they had intentionally declared themselves homeless.

Mr. Justice Michael Nolan decided yesterday that in the 'highly unusual circumstances' he would allow the family to challenge the council's ruling.

But he said that having read the court papers he had reached his decision with 'some misgivings.' Now the full facts about the haunting of No 124 will be revealed at a later court hearing.

The Costellos, who have been staying at a guest house since fleeing last May, were not in court to hear their counsel Mr. David Watkinson outline the 'exceptional circumstances' of the case.

He claimed the council had a duty under the 1985 Housing Act to inquire into the facts of the case

'Doors open, lights go off'

which was supported by independent witnesses.

The council, he said, had acted unlawfully and he wanted their decision quashed.

Mr. Watkinson said the trouble started when another daughter, Sharon, who now lives in a special home for the autistic, was brought to her knees by the sound of heartbeats in the house.

After that the family all experienced ghostly happenings.

A spirtualist pronounced that there were five spirits in the house, one of which was mischievous. A visit from a priest failed to help.

After the family's hurried departure, the council insisted it would have been reasonable for them to stay in the house.

Since August, Jimmy and Sandra Cotterill have lived in the house with their three children - and also suffered unnerving experiences.

Mr. Cotterill, 36 and unemployed, said: 'I have woken in the morning to find front and back doors wide open. Gas fires have been mysteriously turned on, and lights flick on and off. I think the house must still be haunted. The previous tenants had put circles with crosses on top of them on the walls to exorcise ghosts.

"I try to rub them out but they keep reappearing. I am going to see the vicar to ask for his advice. But I am not moving and I have not asked to be rehoused."

EVERYONE HAS THE CHANCE OF A GHOST

by Graham Duffill

THE spirits of No 124 are not alone in preferring the homely surroundings of the surburban street or council estate.

Mrs. Margaret Linton and her three daughters fled their council semi in Wolverhampton after three years of ghostly goings-on, including knocking on the walls and self-switching electric lights. Her daughter Shirely said she was pushed downstairs by an invisible pair of cold, clammy hands.

Four priests with candles and a cross were called in to exorcise the terror of 55 Winteringham Road, Grimsby, where the ghostly figure of a man had been haunting the Currier family. And an astronomy professor experienced the flying objects terrorising the Grieve family in their Glasgow council house.

Worried

Poltergeists are said to be mischievous but harmless spirits, as a rule. They are fond of moving furniture, throwing things and interfering electrical gadgets. Experts say far more homes are haunted than their occupants will admit.

They believe most people are worried about property values and what the neighbours might think if they start talking about their uninvited guests.

The Psychical Research Society now have more than 500 investigators. One said: 'Many people come to us pleading for secrecy. They are almost as scared their friends will laugh at them as they are of the poltergeists.'

ASSIGNMENT 3

Study the *mystery photographs* below and decide whether you think they are real or not.

MYSTERY PHOTOGRAPHS

People believe photographs because cameras 'do not lie.' Yet the spirit pictures that were once all the rage have nearly all shown to be faked. Photographs of ghosts that have not been tampered with at all are the hardest to understand. If ghosts are psychic images, then how can ordinary photographic film record them? Yet all of these pictures are considered by experts to be genuine.

The ghost of Raynham Hall was believed to have the shape of a woman. In 1936 came startling proof. The photographer was setting up his equipment at the foot of the stairs. He saw a phantom drifting down them and took the picture shown right.

This picture is one of the most puzzling ghost photographs ever taken. The woman in the back seat was supposed to be in her grave when the photograph was taken. The driver's wife took this picture of her husband sitting in the car. She claims there was nobody in the car except her husband. Yet the photograph clearly shows the figure of a woman - her mother - who had died a week before. Experts say that the film has not been altered in any way. Yet if you look closely you will see that the corner of her scarf seems to overlap the side pillar of the car. This would only be possible if her face was placed in the picture after it was taken. Yet if the experts are correct and the photograph is genuine, there is no explanation for how it could have happened - unless the woman in the back was a ghost.

People commonly claim to see the ghosts of nuns and priests in churches. Often they are said to stand at or near the altar, praying. The photograph left of a cowled monk standing by an alter rail was taken in the early 1960's by the vicar of a church in England. At the time he saw nothing that was out of the ordinary. But his developed film showed the tall phantom monk seen here. It appears to be about three metres tall. The film was carefully checked by photographic experts but showed no signs of tampering.

Read the extract *Ghostbuster Shatters the Myths About Phantoms*. Then answer these questions.

1 Look at the first three paragraphs. What caused the ghostly music?

2 How much of paranormal activity does Andrew Green say can be explained?

3 What examples of poltergeist activity are given?

4 What does Andrew Green think of these occurrences and their cause?

5 In the second column, what, according to Mr Green, causes ghosts?

6 What are 'living' ones? Give an example of them from the passage.

7 What have you learnt about ghosts from the passage? Do you believe in their existence or not?

GHOSTBUSTER SHATTERS THE MYTHS ABOUT PHANTOMS

by JACK PLEASANT

GHOSTLY piano music in the middle of the night was terrifying the occupants of an old house.

Ghost-hunter Andrew Green soon solved the mystery. His clues were mouse droppings and rodent teeth marks inside the piano. He was convinced that mice gnawing felt pads attached to the piano wires were causing the "music".

He was proved right when a few traps caught the culprits and their nightly performances ceased.

"As much as 98 per cent of the hundreds of ghost investigations I've carried out have proved to have non-occult explanations," said Mr. Green as we chatted in his old cottage, appropriately next to the churchyard at Mountfield in East Sussex. "Once, four reports from motorists claiming to have seen a ghost at a particular spot turned out to be simply a woman's dress left out on a clothes line."

It's that inexplicable two per cent that intrigue him. Like poltergeist activity.

The frighteningly violent effects of this type of haunting have been experienced by several people, particularly families with adolescent children.

"On one startling occasion, I actually watched a bowl of oranges rise unaided off a sideboard," claims the ghost-hunter. "The bowl then shattered into pieces and oranges bounced all around the room."

"In another investigation, the family involved and I saw a heavy clock move from one end of the mantlepiece to the other and back again."

"But I'm personally convinced that such occurrences have nothing to do with the spirits of the dead. I believe they are caused by a type of energy we don't yet understand which is generated by intense human emotions."

The typical poltergeist situation, he says, is a family recently moved into a council house. The husband and wife are probably worried about having to change jobs and shortage of money because of the expense of moving. The young children are nervously trying to settle into new schools.

It all adds up to a tense, emotional atmosphere - and such peculiar effects as he witnessed himself.

Not that Mr. Green disbelieves in ghosts or that some people see them.

It's simply that they are just electro-magnetism, he says, electrical impulses given off by people at times of stress such as murder or suicide.

Somehow, this electrical energy remains in the area and from time to time manifests itself in the form of an image.

Seeming to support his belief that ghosts are not spirits of the dead, are his experiences with "living" ones.

"I've investigated a number of cases where people have seen ghost-like figures of individuals who were very much alive at the time, though elsewhere," he says. "Some people

running an old bakery reported seeing a ghostly shape by the ovens on a number of occasions.

"Significantly, these sightings had only started after an old man who had worked in the bakery for many years had retired. When he died some months later, they ceased. I believe that after his retirement the old man had sat around with his former workplace constantly in his thoughts, mentally going through the tasks he used to perform there."

"So strong was his yearning to be back there that in some strange way his image was projected there. When he died, the cause of the 'haunting' no longer existed and it stopped."

He has even been called out to investigate ghostly smells. Like the posh London dental surgery where staff and patients often smelt bacon and eggs. There were no kitchens near enough to explain it.

But the surgery had once been, Green discovered, the kitchen of a big house.

"It seems possible," he says, "that the hundreds of rashers of bacon and eggs cooked there years before had impregnated their smell in the chimney."

As well as the sophisticated equipment he uses for ghost-hunting, such as tape-recorders, infra-red cameras and thermometers, he usually takes along a ruler and a bag of flour.

"The flour is to detect human footprints if I think a hoax is being carried out," he says.

ASSIGNMENT ⑤

Read *Ghostbuster Shatters the Myths About Phantoms* again. What investigations would you carry out in the council house if you were Mr Green? Can you think of any possible natural causes for some of the things described there? Write a report for the Society for Psychical Research magazine, outlining how you would conduct such an investigation and highlighting what you would expect to discover.

■ This is to be a thorough piece of work and will need planning. Script the story part well. Certain stories may allow for you to have a narrator and pupils to play the part of characters in the story.

You will be able to explain exactly how you feel about the subject of ghosts and whether you believe they exist or not.

ASSIGNMENT ⑥

What would the Society for Psychical Research say about Mr Green's theory of haunted council houses? Write a letter from this society to the editor of the magazine. The article *No, You Can't Walk Out On a Poltergeist*.

Note: *The Society for Psychical Research is a Society that was founded to investigate paranormal happenings. Members are not necessarily believers or disbelievers in ghosts. They like to be regarded as a serious scientific research group.*

ASSIGNMENT ⑦

Try to find out as much as you can about local ghosts and ghost stories. (You could make these stories up and this could form some imaginative coursework.) Discuss the research work that you have been involved in. As a group you are going to tape a radio programe called **Ghost Hour**. The hour should be made up of a few ghost stories followed by a discussion about ghosts and the evidence that supports or refutes their existence.

ASSIGNMENT ⑧

Prepare and write a 5 minute talk to your class about ghosts and why you believe or disbelieve in them.

INFORMATION WAS OBTAINED FROM:

■ Incorporated Society For Psychical Research. 1 Adam and Eve Mews, London.
■ Institute of Psycophysical Research. 118 Banbury Road, Oxford.
■ Committee for the Scientific Investigation of Claims of the Paranormal. 10 Crescent View, Loughton, Essex.
■ The Ghost Club. 93, Muswell Hill, London N10 2QG.

CHAPTER 11

meat or not

ASSIGNMENT ①

Read the following poem carefully

Discuss the poem in your group and think about the questions below. The questions will help you to understand the poem.

The poem is in favour of vegetarianism.

1 Why does the poet say 'We are the living graves of murdered beasts'. What do you think he means by this?

2 Think about the terms used. Why are we 'living graves' and why are the beasts 'murdered'?

3 Does the poet think that animals have rights?

4 How do we take away the rights of animals?

5 Why is Sunday mentioned? What light is the poet talking about?

6 Why does the poet then talk about war? What has war to do with his argument?

LIVING GRAVES

We are the living graves of murdered beasts,
Slaughtered to satisfy our appetites.
We never pause to wonder at our feasts,
If animals, like men, can possibly have rights.
We pray on Sundays that we may have light,
To guide our footsteps on the path we tread.
We're sick of War, we do not want to fight-
The thought of it now fills our hearts with dread,
And yet - we gorge ourselves upon the dead.

Like carrion crows, we live and feed on meat,
Regardless of the suffering and pain,
We cause by doing so, if thus we treat
Defenceless animals for sport or gain,
How can we hope in this world to attain
The PEACE we say we are do anxious for.
We pray for it, o'er hecatombs of slain,
To God while outraging the moral law,
Thus cruelty begets its offspring — WAR.

GEORGE BERNARD SHAW.

What do you think was the most repulsive to his audience at the time – war or eating meat?

Why are carrion crows mentioned?

How are the eating of meat and war connected as far as the poet is concerned?

Look at the language used by the poet. Is there anything unusual about his choice of words?

11 Read the poem again. Try to make sure that you have understood it fully.

Write about one page explaining what the poem was about and how the poet tried to get the message across to the reader.

Meat - Britain's Favourite

We British really enjoy our meat. We always have. 98% of us sit down to meat meals regularly, and figures show that more of us will be eating meat in 1988 than ever before.

Why, because there's more to meat. More taste. More goodness. More convenience. More value. And as our tastes in food have changed, so butchers and supermarkets have kept pace, offering us leaner well trimmed and boneless cuts.

Meat tastes good. Even the smell of a good British roast, sizzling grilled steak, hearty casserole or trendy stirfry can set those taste buds twitching.

Meat does you good. If you want to give your family a well balanced diet make sure they enjoy the nutritional benefits of meat: protein for strong, healthy growth and body building; iron for healthy blood; zinc, vital for healing processes; vitamin B12, which helps prevent anaemia; thiamin, niacin and riboflavin for the conversion of carbohydrates into energy.

Meat is so convenient. With many cuts available for grilling, stirfrying and microwaving, you can have a super meal on the table in minutes. Slower cooking casseroles and stews are wonderfully easy to prepare, especially when you use ready cubed or minced lamb, beef or pork. Whatever you're looking for, you'll find a meaty meal to suit your taste – and your pocket.

from beef lamb
pork
bacon
sausages
other
meat
products
77% from other sources

from other sources, which include eggs, fish & poultry

10% / 41% from dairy products
23% from meats & meat products
7% / 19% from other oils & fats
cakes & biscuits

SOURCES OF
SATURATED FAT IN
THE DOMESTIC
PURCHASES (NFS, 1985)

Meat meals are packed with goodness – great for growing children.

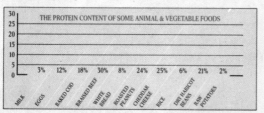

Meat is great value for money. Even after inflation, meat and bacon still cost almost 20% less than in the early 1970s.

Less fat needn't mean less meat. You and your family don't have to go without meat just because you're trying to cut down on fat in food. As you can see from the diagram, many other products contain fat too. What's more, there's always plenty of lean, well trimmed meat in the shops, and you can further reduce the fat content by grilling instead of frying. So give the family meat. It tastes good and it does them good.

THE PROTEIN CONTENT OF SOME ANIMAL & VEGETABLE FOODS
30
25
20
15
10
5
0
3% 12% 18% 30% 8% 24% 25% 6% 21% 2%
MILK EGGS BAKED COD BRAISED BEEF WHITE BREAD ROASTED PEANUTS CHEDDAR CHEESE RICE DRY HARICOT BEANS RAW POTATOES

The protein in lamb, beef and pork compares very well with other foods. For a real meal – there's more to meat.

Source: The Meat & Livestock Commission

ASSIGNMENT ②

Read *Meat Britain's Favourite* on page 101.

Design an advertisement that is titled **Meat is Good for You** and that is specifically aimed at young, growing children.

Vegetarians could design an advertisement advocating a meat-free diet.

Both advertisements should emphasise the health issues involved.

Vegetarians will be helped by reading the article *One Child's Meat*.

ASSIGNMENT ③

Read *One Child's Meat* and *The Ethical Dimension*.

Then draw two columns down the page, one headed **Meat** and the other **Vegetarianism.** List an arguments in favour of either in the correc columns.

Add to this list as you get more information furthe into the chapter. This will help you later.

THE ETHICAL DIMENSION

Claims are made that vegetarians and vegans are healthier than meat eaters. They may well be because most of them are obviously more concerned about their diet and health than the rest of the population; they may eat less in total, be less likely to smoke and take more exercise, for example. Better health cannot be ascribed to avoidance of meat eating alone unless fit, non-smokers adopting a low-fat, high-fibre diet containing lean meat are compared with similar people deriving similar proportions of fat, proteins, vitamins and minerals from other sources.

Adoption of a vegetarian regime frequently leaves people consuming a high level of saturated fat. The Vegetarian Society launched its Cordon Vert Cookery courses with a press release that featured a dish called Brazilian Bake. This dish derived 77 per cent of its calories from fat, its content of saturated fat per 100g was three times that of lean beef!

There is no doubt that we are in a phase where, because of the communications explosion, more and more people are exposed to vegetarian arguments, both moral and peripheral. Local radio stations provide a platform for local societies; magazines like to catalogue personalities - particularly pop personalities - who have adopted vegetarianism and to feature athletes who achieve excellent performances on a vegetarian diet.

Athletes who achieve world-record performances on diets that include red meat (even pies and sausages) seldom have their diet mentioned. When Ivan Lendl was winning rounds at Wimbledon, the papers described each success as another demonstration of the benefits of a vegetarian diet - when Boris Becker finally won, not one put it down to the dietary benefits of wurst! Kirsty McDermott's 1,000m record was described as "...... another useful commercial for the vegetarian diet", this happened on a day Steve Cram did not break a world record - he missed by 0.67 seconds and was presumably regarded as a 'hamburger-has-been.'

Source: The Meat and Livestock Commission

One Child's Meat

If your child decides to become a vegetarian, should you worry about vitamins and minerals? **Heather Kirby** reports

When Andrew Tallis was just a toddler sitting in a supermarket trolley, he asked a friend of his mother's who was pushing him round, what all that stuff in the freezer was. Thinking his mother would want him to be given an honest answer, the friend said it was chopped-up dead pigs and dead chicken and that's what people ate. Andrew, who is now eight years old, has been a strict vegetarians ever since.

"I tried to coax him out of it at first" sayes his mother, Mary Tallis, 28, a student at Manchester Polytechnic. "Then I believed it was something that would pass, but when he was three I bought a packet of fish fingers, because all children liked those, and he point-blank refused to eat any. Then he started to ask me what was in any packet or tinned food I bought. When he learned to read at five he checked himself.

"Now, I'm a vegetarian, too, because it was just too much bother preparing two meals, although my husband James still eats meat that he cooks for himself."

Andrew is not so unusual. Small children often turn a tortured face from plate to parent when they make the connection between meat and animals. Mealtimes are a notorious breeding ground for conflict, for most parents try their best to accommodate children whatever their latest food fad is - and today's parent is concerned with health, not power.

What families are increasingly having to cope with now is pressure from the new generation of highly articulate teenagers who are being made to think about the advantages and disadvantages of meat eating and meat production as butchers and vegetarians lobby for their support.

A Gallup survey conducted at the end of last year on behalf of the Realeat Company which makes vege burgers and vege bangers showed that one-third of this country's 4.3 million non-meat eaters are now children under 16. And a survey to be published next week by the Vegetarian Society indicates that because of pressure from students, 95 per cent of British universities, colleges and polytechnics are now providing vegetarian meals. In some student restaurants, more than one in five of the meals served are vegetarian.

The trend towards vegetarianism is being led by women, who are now twice as likely to be non-meat eating as men. But for non-vegetarian parents the arguments impressionable childen bring home ignite a little timebomb that is ticking away in the kitchen. Even if parents have sympathy with the arguments, what they worry about is whether giving up protein-rich meat is safe for a body that still has a lot of growing to do.

According to Dr. Tom Sanders, lecturer in nutrition at King's College, London and an authority on the growth and development of vegetarian children, we need not worry if our offspring suddenly take it into their heads to give up meat. "One starts off life as a vegetarian, taking in only milk and cereal; so long as there are dairy products and a variety of other foods in the diet, vegetarian children can grow up just as healthy as omnivores."

Sanders, a meat-eater himself, says: "Problems come about when children go on to veganism and want to cut out milk and cheese altogether - then they have to avoid Vitamin B12 deficiency by taking supplements. Vegan children can still grow ok, although they are small in size and light in weight, but I'm not going to say that is harmful."

A collaborative study of the effects of the fibre contents of diet on bowel function and health in general by Professor John Dickerson, head of the division of nutrition and food science in the Department of Biochemistry at the University of Surrey, and Dr. Jill Davies, a senior lecturer in the Home Economics and Consumer Studies Department at South Bank Polytechnic, showed that lifelong vegetarians are healthier than meat-eaters.

"We discovered that certain diseases, like appendicitis, irritable bowel syndrome, haemorrhoids, varicose veins and constipation occurred more often among omnivores, and that the age at which they occurred was much earlier than in vegetarians," Davies says.

"Compared with omnivores, vegetarians had made only 22 per cent of the visits to hospital out-patients and had spent a similar proportion of the time in hospital. Converted into economic terms, the lifelong vegetarians we studied cost the NHS £12,340 compared with the omnivores' £58,062."

Davies adds: "I am not a vegetarian, but what our study showed is that vegetarianism is very healthy and would be good for children so long as their diet is very carefully planned. People often speak defensively about vegetarianism and a lot of nonsense is talked about vitamin deficiency. Take iron - most of it comes from plant sources, and because vegetarians eat a lot of fruit their intake of vitamin C will increase their ability to absorbe iron."

Dr. Michael Turner, the former director general of the British Nutrition Foundation and now a consultant nutritionist, worries that teenagers may not have enough nutritional knowledge to ensure that a new regime has adequate nutrients, "I think parents should insist that their children make the change gradually to give them time to find out what are the right things to eat so that the body can adjust."

Janet Lambert, a nutritionist with the Meat and Livestock Commissions, claims that "In terms of 100 calories consumed, you get a lot more nutrients from meat than other foods. Evidence of the number of children who are becoming vegetarian is a bit vague. You're not allowed to interview children so the Gallup survey has come from parents."

The Vegetarian Society is currently running a campaign called SCREAM, School Campaign for Reaction Against Meat, which the campaign co-ordinator, Graham Clarke, claims was launched as an antidote to the meat industry's Adopt a Butcher advertising. Part of the campaign is a powerful half-hour video, which shows the inside of an abattoir and a cow being shot in the head.

It is hardly surprising that after this short, sharp, shock treatment many youngsters annouce their conversion. Typical of what tends to happen next is explained by Barbara Humber, headmistress of Glendower Prep School in South Kensington: "My daughter Nicki decided to become a vegetarian when she was 14, but my husband and I remain carnivores. It can be a bit of a bore making two separate meals."

The accusation that the Vegetarian Soceity is bent on indoctrinating children is dismissed as patronizing by 17-year-old Chris Davies, a pupil at Bromsgrove High School in Worcestershire, and a vegetarian. "I don't think people of my generation can be indoctrinated that easily," he sayš. "I think it is healthier to be a vegetarian. I used to drink milk and eat cheese and eggs until I read an article recently about the cruelty inherent in milk production. Now I've given all those up, too, but I'm still very healthy."

Healthy, but only because his mother, teacher Margot Davies, has taken a lot of time and trouble to find out about the right alternative foods for him. "We were quite worried at first when he announced it, not because of the inconvenience, but about whether he would be getting the right sort of protein." she says. "You have to be prepared to do quite a bit of forward planning - particularly when you're a full-time working mother.

"Vegetarian cheese is very expensive, and soya milk costs more than ordinary milk and we can't get it delivered. Chris is entitled to his views and I don't want mealtimes turned into a battleground. He hasn't tried to convert us, but when we go out for a meal now we choose a vegetarian restaurant."

ASSIGNMENT ❹

Look at *Teaching the Sins of the Flesh.*

What is the article about?

How easily would your group be influenced by a talk or video similar to that discussed?

What facts were presented to persuade children to become vegetarian?

Do you believe any information presented by SCREAM? What do you believe?

Why is the writer upset? Do you think both sides of an issue should be presented to pupils? Why?

Can you list/recognise any arguments that vegetarians could use as to why they are vegetarian?

What arguments could meat eaters counter these with?

WOMEN

Teaching the sins of the flesh

Violet Johnstone on a campaign to remove meat from the schoolchild's curriculum

The steady growth in vegetarianism is being given a sudden boost with a campaign which is proving highly successful in schools. While more adults are turning to vegetarian diets for health reasons, their offspring are far more likely to be converted on the grounds of cruelty to animals.

Maybe your children have already come back asking for veggieburgers or chunky nut roasts if they have seen the video, *The Vegetarian World*, which should get an Oscar for effective propaganda. Many children will feel an instant affinity with the little girl who says simply, "I'm a vegetarian because I love animals"; all will squirm at the sight of knives being plunged into the throats of chickens hanging helplessly upside down as they wait for slaughter.

Scream!, the School Campaign for Reaction Against Meat, is the new youth pressure group of the Vegetarian Society, which is sending information packs on the "real horrors of factory farming and abuse of animals" into schools, and offering to give talks and show a video on the subject. Emotive stuff.

Leaflets give vivid descriptions of fluffy chicks having the end of their beaks hacked off so that they will not peck each other to death as they grow, crammed together, in tiny cages, and of sows dragged back to the "rape rack" five days after their piglets are weaned at two weeks. (It's unfortunate that the picture of the pig stall on one leaflet should be 13 years old.)

A small green booklet, *The A to Z of Vegetarianism*, has powerful messages for young people very open to persuasion. Under "H" for Health, children are told: "It has been proven that vegetarians suffer much less from heart disease, diabetes, bowel cancer and many other fatal illnesses. Under "S" for School Dinners, "Remember, it is your right to have vegetarian food at school and it should be provided".

(The evidence for vegetarians suffering fewer diseases is based solely on studies from religious groups such as the Seventh Day Adventists. So far no study among the general public can substantiate the Vegetarian Society's claims. For reasons that are not known, all religious sects seem to have low rates of certain diseases, irrespective of whether or not they eat meat and dairy products. No child has the "right" to vegetarian food at school, where meals are at the discretion of individual local education authorities.)

The video is aimed at children of 13 upwards, and the Society is making another for primary schools. "Children tend to be more sympathetic than adults," says Juliet Gellatley, the Society's Youth Education Officer, "They do things by gradual process. They'll give up meat, then fish, then leather shoes." It is natural that they then become vegan, she says,

At Bishop Heber High School, near Chester, Ms Gellatley "swayed many pupils", says Dr Paul Fenwick, the biology teacher. "The children were very distressed by the film they saw. The slaughter of animals didn't go down well." He admitted that no talk putting forward the other point of view was being planned.

It was the same at Davenport School in Stockport, where Ms Gellatley is giving four talks. "Nobody has approached us so we are not having a speaker 'from the other side', though it would be a good idea - farmers are too busy, I suppose," says Eileen Howarth, home economics teacher.

The National Farmer's Union says its policy is to encourage farmers to give talks, but that it doesn't have a school programme as such. "If people don't want to eat meat you can't do anything about it," said the spokeswoman.

Other organisations produce good, balanced literature but are unwilling to get involved in any hard-hitting campaign. The Meat and Livestock Commission says firmly that it wouldn't adopt the same approach as the Vegetarian Society, but is successful in many school projects. For example, it will sponsor children who eat a school meal containing meat to the tune of 10p per meal for, say, a week and give the money to charity.

The Association of Agriculture maintains it just hasn't the funds to send speakers into schools. Common sense does prevail, it says; 75 per cent of teachers would recognise Scream! as propaganda.

However, with its school campaign the Vegetarian Society is bringing the issue of intensive farming to children's notice and it seems a shame that no one is putting forward the other side of this picture. Roger Ewbank of the Universities Federation for Animal Welfare, which aims to speak to students but does sometimes talk to sixth forms, says that many of the concerns are correct.

"But what is the alternative to battery birds if society wants eggs and poultry produced under hygienic conditions at prices it can afford to pay? The Ministry of Agriculture has a unit in Cleethorpes looking at aviary and perchary systems indoors, but where birds have a social life and can jump from perch to perch, and where there's an impression of living going on. But such units are more difficult to run."

He points out that there is a higher incidence of disease among free range birds.

Doesn't this make good school debating material?

Source: The Sunday Telegraph 1/11/87

ASSIGNMENT ⑤

You are a parent of a fourth form pupil. This week the school was visited by a representative of SCREAM who showed your child and others a video about vegetarianism and gave a talk on the subject.

Your child has now become a vegetarian and refused to eat meat or any meat products. As your husband is a butcher this is particularly awkward.

Write a letter to the school explaining the situation and also complaining about the showing of the film. You must give reasons for your views.

- You may wish to point out that meat is regarded as healthy and necessary for growing children.
- You feel that both sides of the argument should have been presented.
- You would like to be consulted about whether you wish your children to see films of this kind.
  Is it propaganda?

ASSIGNMENT ⑥

You have decided to become vegetarian and have to persuade your parents to respect your wishes.

Write out the conversation that is likely to take place between you and your parents over this issue.

Your intention must be to persuade them to allow *you* to become a vegetarian using arguments that you have already come across, as well as some of your own that you may have. You are not trying to change *their* eating habits.

- Your diet of fresh fruit and more vegetables could add to the food bill a little. However, meat is expensive also and you won't be eating that.

- Vegetarians can buy easy-to-use packet mixes like lentil roasts, veggie burgers – so meals can be just as quick to make.

- Protein requirements can be adequately provided using nuts, grains and pulses like soya beans and so on.
- Look at the following three posters. Baked beans on toast is a vegetarian dish!

Put less of your money where your mouth is.

You know the cost of meat is rising all the time ~ how much longer can you rise to meet it ?
Doctors have said we should cut our meat eating by 15% for the sake of our health. Why not cut out more, for the sake of your health ~ and your purse.

The Vegetarian Society, 53 Marloes Road, London W8 6L

BY THE TIME YOU'VE FINISHED READING THIS HEADLINE 520 ANIMALS HAVE BEEN SLAUGHTERED FOR FOOD

"There are laws, regulations and inspectors...."
"We're supposed to be a nation of animal lovers ~ surely they don't let the animals suffer ?"
"Aren't they put to sleep like pets ?"

Well, no.
Conditions in slaughterhouses are bloody and barbaric. Why not visit your local slaughterhouse to see how your Sunday roast ended its life ? Don't fancy it ? It's something most people would rather not think about. If it worries you, think instead about the alternative ~ a meat free diet. It's healthy, cheap and humane.

By now, a further 1,500 animals are dead......or dying.

The Vegetarian Society, 53 Marloes Road, London W8 6LA

LET THE FROGS KEEP THEIR LEGS

CIWF

Tel. 0730 64208

COMPASSION IN WORLD FARMING · PETERSFIELD · HANTS · GU32 3EW

ASSIGNMENT ⑦

Look carefully at the posters on page 106, the cartoons and *World Tragedy* below, and the posters, *The World Holds Enough . . .* and *Human Hunger* on page 108. In your groups establish exactly what connections these articles make between meat-eating and world hunger. Is it the only reason for world hunger?

Ian Kellas/Oxfam
Source: Oxfam

WORLD TRAGEDY: 300 Jumbo Jet Crashes EVERY DAY

Assoc. Press

Over **500 million** people on this planet are severely undernourished, and **40 million** die each year from starvation or hunger-related diseases. That is the equivalent of 300 Jumbo Jet crashes every day, **with no survivors**.

Source: The Vegan Society

The world holds

'enough for every man's need but not for every man's greed' Mahatma Gandhi

WHEN YOU ARE VEGETARIAN
WE CAN LIVE

HUMAN HUNGER

It is often argued that vegetarians care more about animals than humans. Yet many people decide to become vegetarians precisely because they are concerned about hunger in the Third World.

At least ten times more people can be sustained on vegetarian food than on a diet based on meat (see illustration).

The present population of Britain is 56 million (approx). If everyone ate a balanced and nutritious vegetarian diet we could feed a population of approximately **250** million.

At present more than 90% of our agricultural land is used to grow feed for farm animals, instead of food for humans. Worse still, every year we import potential famine-relief food to feed farm animals. Most of this food is wasted in their digestive system.

10 ACRES (5 football pitches) will support—

61 people
growing SOYA

24 people
growing WHEAT

10 people
growing MAIZE

2 people
growing CATTLE

reproduced
by courtesy of the Vegetarian Society

...ansion of the yield of supplies of vegetable origin is essential
Food for a Future)

ASSIGNMENT 8

Decide as a group whether you are in favour of a vegetarian or a meat-eating diet. You are going to advertise a **Meat-Free** or a **Meat-Eating Day** over the radio. Your advertisement will obviously have to highlight the virtues of your chosen diet. Plan your campaign well and then tape on to cassette your advertisement for this event.

As a class you should spend time listening to each other's attempts, to see what constitutes a good appeal and why.

If you are in favour of meat eating:

- Extol the virtues of meat as a healthy food. Is it natural for us to eat meat?
- There are a range of delicious dishes available to meat eaters.
- What would you miss if you couldn't eat meat?
- Eating vegetarian food can be more expensive.
- Find out the price of meat to substantiate some of your ideas.
- Finally read the information in favour of meat eating again.
- Look at the notes you made earlier.

If you are in favour of a vegetarian diet:

- You could argue the case on moral grounds.
- Think about the Third World material you have been given: Is a vegetarian diet healthier?
- What evidence could you include?
- Give some information about the range of food available.
- Look at prices of vegetarian foods. Are they cheaper than eating meat?
- Finally read the information in favour of vegetarianism again. Look at the notes you made earlier.

ASSIGNMENT 9

Choose one of the following essay titles and write approximately 400–500 words. Remember to plan your essay well and always back your ideas up with facts: 'I think this because . . '

 Gandhi said 'The World has enough for every man's need but not for every man's greed'. If we all became vegetarian then the world would have enough to eat. Do you agree with this point of view and is it a good enough reason to give up meat?

2 You have been asked to write a speech for a school public speaking competition either for or against vegetarianism. Write the speech you would give.

3 'The Lion might be the King of the Jungle but Man and Womankind are the Emperors and Empresses of the whole World. Animals are there to provide sustenance for us and we have every right to use them in this way. Why did God give us tools, weapons and the power to use them if this wasn't true? I think the whole idea of vegetarianism is a load of bunkum. If we were supposed to eat vegetables and fruit we would have been made in the image of rabbits, or better still monkeys and not in the image of God!' With your reasons give your views on this writer's feelings.

INFORMATION WAS OBTAINED FROM:

- Animal Aid. 7 Castle Street, Tonbridge, Kent.
- Compassion in World Farming. Petersfield, Hants GU32 3EW.
- The Vegetarian Society. 53 Marloes Road, London W8 6LA
- The Vegan Society Ltd. 33-35 George Street, Oxford OX1 2AY
- OXFAM. Consult your local telephone directory for details
- Meat and Livestock Commission. P.O. Box 44, Queensway House, Bletchley MK2 2EF

CHAPTER 12

capital punishment

ASSIGNMENT 1

Read a newspaper every day for a week before you begin this work. Cut out all articles that deal with violent crimes like rape, armed raids, attacks on old people and children and all cases of murder.

ASSIGNMENT 2

Look carefully at the material you have collected. Try to group crimes together according to their nature. Make a chart of your findings. Note also any sentences meted out by the courts to criminals involved in violent crimes.

- Are you shocked by the amount of crime reported?
- Is there less than you anticipated?
- What view do you get of this country?
- Are we a violent nation?
- What do you think of the sentences that are being given?
- All violent crime is bad but we still find some crimes more shocking and upsetting than others. Which annoy and upset you the most?

ASSIGNMENT 3

Read the following poem and discuss it as well as your immediate reactions to the material you have found.

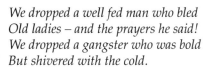

BALLAD OF THE LONG DROP

We dropped a chap that raped a child:
He gave no trouble, kind and mild.
We dropped a kid that killed a cop:
He made a lightish drop.

We dropped a well fed man who bled
Old ladies – and the prayers he said!
We dropped a gangster who was bold
But shivered with the cold.

We dropped a gentlemanly rake
Who said it wasn't our mistake
We dropped a fool or two who tried
To struggle as they died.

We dropped a lad who killed by whim,
Who cursed us as we pinioned him.
We dropped a girl who shot a bloke
Because her heart was broke.

Her heart was broke. She did him in
For love: but love like hers is sin.
We dropped her, for we drop them straight
For love as well as hate.

For love as well as hate we serve
To break the neck and break the nerve
Of those who break the laws of man:
We serve you all as best we can.

JOHN PUDNEY

I THINK THAT . . .

I AM ALL IN FAVOUR OF HANGING RAPISTS, SINCE IT SEEMS THAT WE'RE NOW BREEDING A NATION OF THEM. I LIVE ON A NAVAL ESTATE AND THERE HAVE BEEN MANY INCIDENTS IN THE AREA INVOLVING CHILDREN. NO WONDER MOST PEOPLE ARE TALKING OF EMIGRATING – WE'LL CERTAINLY GO UNLESS HANGING IS RE-INTRODUCED. THIS MUST BE THE SOFTEST AND MOST LAUGHED AT COUNTRY IN THE WORLD.

MRS E.M.KIDD, IPSWICH

IF CAPITAL PUNISHMENT WERE RESTORED, THAT WOULD BE THE BIGGEST PROOF OF ALL THAT ENGLAND IS GOING BACK TO THE 19th CENTURY. I'D BECOME EVEN MORE ASHAMED OF THIS COUNTRY.

R.SWAIN, LEICESTER.

TO EXECUTE ONE TO DETER ANOTHER SEEMS TO ME TO BE INDEFENSIBLE.

RT. HON ROY HATTERSLEY, MP, MAY, 1982 DEBATE COL 683

WE MUST RECOGNISE THAT IF WE REALLY ARE TO TACKLE THE PENAL PROBLEMS OF THE COUNTRY WE MUST TURN OUR ATTENTION TO THAT, INSTEAD OF AUTOMATICALLY SAYING THAT THE ANSWER IS HANGING AND FLOGGING.

THE RT HON EDWARD HEATH DURING THE 1983 COMMONS DEBATE

I FAVOUR HANGING FOR RAPE AND MURDER. LIKE THOUSANDS OF OTHERS, I CANNOT UNDER-STAND WHY OUR GOVERNMENT WON'T LISTEN TO THE DEMANDS OF THE PEOPLE THEY ARE ELECTED TO SERVE. HANGING IS NO MORE OUTDATED AND BARBARIC THAN RAPE AND MURDER.

MRS R.A.BARBER, PETERBOROUGH

❛ It is curious, but till that moment I had never realized what it means to destroy a healthy, conscious man. When I saw the prisoner step aside to avoid the puddle I saw the mystery, the unspeakable wrongness, of cutting a life short when it is in full tide. This man was not dying, he was alive just as we are alive. All the organs of his body were working – bowels digesting food, skin renewing itself, nails growing, tissues forming – all toiling away in solemn foolery. His nails would still be growing when he stood on the drop, when he was falling through the air with a tenth of a second to live. His eyes saw the yellow gravel and the grey walls, and his brain still remembered, foresaw, reasoned, even about puddles. He and we were a party of men walking together, seeing, hearing, feeling, understanding the same world: and in two minutes, with a sudden snap, one of us would be gone – one less, one world less. ❜

George Orwell : A Hanging, Adelphi, 1931

WOMEN SPEAK WITH ONE VOICE:

THEY ALL DESERVE THE ROPE

Today's readers have flocked to back the recent call by police chief James Anderton for the castration of rapists. More than 65% of the letters received came from women and of the entire postbag only two, both signed by men, disagreed with Greater Manchester's Chief Constable. Mr Anderton has personally received letters of support by the sackload, again mostly from women. The overwhelming majority of those who wrote to Today also voiced extremely strong views in support of the return of hanging, or other forms of capital punishment, for murder and crimes of extreme violence. In a society which rightly condemns murder, it is not then appropriate for the state to sanction the deliberate taking of life as a punishment. There is an underlying hypocrisy in this notion.

Source: Today 22/9/88

HOWARD LEAGUE FOR PENAL REFORM

The Cruelty of Execution

Capital Punishment is cruel and inhumane. The long process involves mental anguish for the offender which amounts to torture. In America prisoners wait for years on death row.

There is no humane way of killing someone.

Hanging causes death by a shock of extreme violence and leaves the body with neck elongated. There are cases where death has not happened at the first attempt, or been instantaneous. The Howard Association's Annual Report 1886 states:

"At the execution of a criminal at Norwich, in December, his head was jerked off his body."

This is but one of the scandalous and horrible executions at that time. The Association goes on to report... *'criminals whose heads have been partially or wholly wrenched from their bodies'* whilst the death struggles of others have been unduly prolonged by bungling mismanagement. In one case the process of execution was attempted several times, and finally had to be abandoned.

Other methods, including electrocution and gassing are no more humane! The use of lethal injection may not work in former drug users or diabetics.

Source: The Havard League for Penal Reform

THE VOICE OF *TODAY*

KILLING WILL NEVER CURE

CALLS to bring back hanging feature strongly in the agenda for next month's Tory party conference But this is no narrow, Tory prejudice.

The 17 resolutions demanding death for murderers reflect the widespread feelings throughout the whole nation. People of every age, class, sex, colour and political leaning are desperate to find ways to stem the tide of violence.

When women don't feel safe to walk down city streets, when children can be savagely assulted even in peaceful country villages and when terrorists and criminals threaten our soldiers and police is it any wonder that people cry out for an answer.

But the death penalty is not the right one. There are several reasons. The risk of hanging an innocent person, for instance. Or the difficulty of deciding which killing deserves the gallows and which does not.

The most important reason though is a moral one. If we condemn

people to death we make the State our agent in a killing just as brutal as a murderer's. We drag ourselves down to their level.

Capital punishment is a form of official revenge no less barbarous than the criminal's slaughter of his victim. The official hangman is no model to set before the people of Britain.

That does not mean we should be soft on killers. On the contary, short of turning killers ourselves we should be as tough as possible.

No remedy should be overlooked. The first priority is to have a police force through whose net no murderer can hope to slip. Then penalties must fit the crime, including life sentences that are exactly that, with no remission and an iron regime of hard labour that criminals learn to fear as intensely as the rope.

Parliament must not bring back hanging. But the government must listen to the fears expressed in the Tory motions - and act to calm them.

ASSIGNMENT ④

Read the material on pages 112 and 113. In two columns write down the reasons why people favour capital punishment and why they oppose it.

Then answer the following question giving three reasons for your answer.

Do you agree with the idea that capital punishment should be reintroduced?

Now look at the material on pages 112 and 113 again. Are there any other reasons to be found above that you could add to those you already have? Are there any reasons given by people who have the opposing view to you that make you a little worried about your standpoint? Why do they worry you?

If you are in favour of capital punishment you should spend some time thinking about exactly what types of crimes this penalty would apply to.

ASSIGNMENT ⑤

Read *Stop This Act Of Folly*.

Note: *Criminals can be held in prison where they come under the jurisdiction of the Home Secretary, the courts, prison service and so on. However, if they are found to be criminally insane they are detained under the Mental Health Act. In these cases they are kept not in prison but in high security mental institutions. Broadmoor is one such institution. Once they are deemed cured they are released on the recommendation of a tribunal made up of doctors, a judge and so on. They are not transferred to prison to complete their sentence. Did you know that when the death penalty was in operation anyone found to be criminally insane could not be sentenced to death?*

Discuss the following questions in your groups.

1. What is the article *Stop This Act of Folly* about?

2. What will the judge, psychiatrist and layman be discussing next month?

3. In what way could people in favour of hanging use information in this article as a reason for its reintroduction?

STOP THIS ACT OF FOLLY

SIXTEEN years ago, the battered body of Shirley Ann Boldy was found in wood near her home in Hemingfield, Yorkshire. She had been raped and then hacked to death with a kitchen knife, after being abducted on her way to school.

Next month, at Park Lane Hospital, Liverpool, three men, a judge, psychiatrist and layman will sit down to decide whether the killer described when convicted as a 'monster' who committed 'sub human' acts on Shirley should be allowed to rejoin society.

Peter Joseph Pickering is now 51. Before he was ordered to be detained without limit of time in Broadmoor in December 1972, he had spent no less than 15 years in prison for attacks on teenage girls.

He killed Shirley only five months after coming out of prison, where he had been serving a nine year sentence for indecency and assaulting a woman.

Source: The Mail on Sunday 16/10/88

CAMPAIGN FOR LAW AND ORDER

Another powerful argument, albeit an expediency, in favour of the death penalty is that the number of prisoners serving so-called life sentences is rapidly increasing. At present there are over 2,000 convicted persons serving "life sentences". This is enormously expensive and the number is bound to increase indefinitely. At present, the cost is estimated at between £400 and £1,000 per week for each "lifer" depending on the amount of security required.

The more vicious and dangerous the criminal, the more it costs to keep him. The risk of escape and further killings in the course of escape attempts are also increasing and the convict has little to lose. The abolition of the death penalty is claimed to be a sign of a civilised society. Try telling that to a mother whose son has been murdered or to the parents of a murdered child.

Source: Campaign for Law and Order

ASSIGNMENT ⑥

Choose to write *one* of the letters outlined below.

1 Imagine that you are the parent of a child who was murdered recently. You desperately wish to see the death penalty restored. Put your case in an open letter to the editor of your local newspaper.

- Look carefully at the article from *Campaign for Law and Order.* Details in this could strengthen your case.
- Refer also to the notes you made earlier.

2 Imagine that your son/daughter is about to be hanged. Write to your local newspaper explaining your feelings about this.

- You will need to include arguments similar to those noted earlier.
- Look at the article *Terrorism*. Information here could also help.

TERRORISM

In the last few years, there have been suggestions that capital punishment might be reintroduced specifically for terrorist offences resulting in death. The main arguments against this proposition are:

1. Terrorists are even less likely to be deterred by capital punishment than other murderers. As a former Home Secretary, Robert Carr (now Lord Carr), said at a meeting in the House of Commons on 20 April 1982:

"They are fanatics who, however perverted they may be in their thinking and feeling, see themselves as fighting for a cause higher than themselves and who are living in a state of mind of dangerous exultation, in which they hold even their own lives at a relatively low price."

It seems unlikely that those who carry explosives, have seen colleagues blown to death when carrying similar explosives and who run the risk of death in their activities would be deterred by the introduction of capital punishment.

2. During the stages of committal, trial, appeal and the days before the execution, terrorists would have a strong motive for taking hostages and threatening to kill them if the accused and convicted men and women were executed, and also for violence against those involved in the process of trial, appeal, imprisonment and execution - namely judge, jury, witnesses, prosecuting counsel, police and prison officers.

3. The experience of other countries suggests that the execution of terrorists would be followed by reprisals.

4. Since capital punishment would not apply to those under 18, the introduction of the death penalty for terrorist offences would reinforce the trend for terrorist organisations to recruit increasingly younger members.

5. The defeat of terrorism involves driving a wedge between the terrorist group and the section of the community which supports it. This is less likely if capital punishment creates a new generation of martyrs.

Source: NACRO

POLICE FEDERATION OF ENGLAND AND WALES
JOINT CENTRAL COMMITTEE

Our policy is that capital punishment should be available to the courts in respect of the crime of murder. We are not seeking for special protection for police officers, although we can prove they have been uniquely affected by the abolition of capital punishment. We do not believe that it is possible to define categories of homicide, and say that some are more deserving of capital punishment than others. Praiseworthy attempts to do this, embodied in the 1957 Homicide Act, threw up so many anomalies that the way was paved for complete abolition in 1965. We believe that each case would have to be decided upon its merits, with mercy being exercised in all appropriate cases.

In the 22 years since abolition, 41 police officers have been killed by criminals in England, Scotland and Wales compared with 14 such deaths in the 22 years before abolition. Each year about 15,000 police officers are assaulted on duty, and about 4,000 sustain injuries which warrant compensation from the Criminal Injuries Compensation Board, and we are particularly concerned about attacks on elderly citizens and on women.

Terrorism has added an awesome dimension to the question of capital punishment. When the House of Commons voted to abolish capital punishment for a five year period in 1965, acts of terrorism in Britain were virtually unknown. The vote to make abolition permanent took place in 1969, just before the present troubles in Northern Ireland degenerated into terrorism. For some time, the United Kingdom has witnessed terrorism on a scale without precedent in our history. An alarming number of people have been killed in Northern Ireland, including officers serving in the Royal Ulster Constabulary, and members of the security forces. Attempts to spread the campaign of bombing and murder to the rest of the United Kingdom have seen the outrages of the Hyde Park, Regents Park and Harrods, Guildford and Birmingham bomb explosions and attacks on the Tower of London and elsewhere. There have also been deliberate attempts in some cases successful, to murder prominent persons who were outspoken in their condemnation of terrorism. Members of Parliament will not need to be reminded that two of their colleagues have been assassinated in recent years.

Britain has also witnessed examples of terrorism perpetrated by murder gangs whose targets have been their opponents in the politics of the Middle East. There have also been hi-jacking incidents at London Airport, and the siege of the Iranian Embassy.

The overwhelming view of the police service is that capital punishment should be restored for the crime of murder. We accept, of course, that there are degrees of murder and we are not saying that all persons who are convicted of homicide should suffer the death penalty. Our belief is that in an increasingly violent society where criminal elements have shown a complete disregard for the sanctity of human life, the State must be empowered to decide that, in some cases, the only adequate punishment for crimes which have outraged society, is the death penalty.

31st July, 1987.

The National Association for the Care and Resettlement of Offenders

There are still many people who believe that only the death penalty can control (or anyway diminish) the growth of terrorism, hijacking, kidnapping and the taking of hostages. There are many, too, who hold that even if it had no effect on those crimes, the death penalty would be appropriate on the "just desserts" principle – the offender deserves hanging even if his death may worsen the general problem.

The National Campaign for the Abolition of Capital Punishment sees the problem in the following terms:

- Great Britain has decided, like most countries, that judicial killing has no place in a civilised state, and that this applies to the execution of terrorists as much as to that of any murderer.

- In any case, the practical arguments against executing terrorists are peculiarly strong. Judicial killing is unavoidably slow. There is a preliminary hearing, a trial, usually one or more appeals against conviction; and it can all take many months – in some countries, years. During that time other coercive crimes are likely to happen, including the taking of hostages whose lives will depend on the fate of the prisoner.
"Terrorism" today is often the work of minors, female as well as male, whom it would be virtually unthinkable to execute. And the death penalty for terrorists of "executionable age" might have the ghastly effect of increasing the use of minors for purpise of homicide.

- Moreover, it makes no sense to kill terrorists whose aims, whatever we think of them, may to them be idealistic, and not to kill those who murder for personal gain.

- Recent years have seen a tragic sequence of convictions against innocent people. With terrorism as with other forms of homicide, there is s constant risk of convictions against innocent people.

- The death penalty, like any other penalty, will deter some killers, but there is no evidence that it does so more than any other. It is in the nature of political "terrorism" that it is the work of fanatics who accept (indeed sometimes relish) the risk of death "for the cause". The judicial killing of terrorists, more often than not, has the opposite effect to that which is intended.

- Reprisals will often follow executions, leading to the loss of still more innocent lives.

ASSIGNMENT 7

Look at the material from the POLICE FEDERATION and NACRO.

Imagine that a debate is taking place in the House of Commons. The subject for debate is the motion that 'Capital Punishment should be reintroduced for terrorists who commit violent attacks on the public and armed forces of this nation'.

Two of the articles you have just read deal with the issue of terrorism. As a group use this information as well as your own ideas to plan and conduct this debate. You will need to appoint one person in favour of and one opposed to the motion. You will also need a chairperson who ensures that the debate is conducted in an orderly manner. Other members of the group will be able to ask questions of the two main speakers. Try taping this debate. Make it as realistic as possible by addressing each other by title and constituency.

ASSIGNMENT 8

Read *Women Speak With One Voice They All Deserve the Rope* and the *Today* article again. Imagine that you are a group of people who have been chosen to decide what sentences people should serve for various crimes of rape and violence.

- Look at the research you did when you started this work. List the different crimes that were reported.
- Now add any other crimes that you can think of that aren't in your list.
- Are there exceptions to any of the sentences you have imposed? Would you treat anyone differently, eg, first time offenders with no prior history of this type of behaviour; children under a certain age; or people who are mentally disturbed?

ASSIGNMENT 9

Write your conclusions above in the form of an official report to the House of Commons. Remember the tone should be formal.

ASSIGNMENT 10

There is to be a referendum to decide whether to reintroduce capital punishment or not. Design a leaflet that sets out to persuade people to your point of view. Whether you choose to support capital punishment or oppose it will depend on the majority decision in your group.

ASSIGNMENT 11

The Bible says that 'Man is made in the image of God and that to kill a man (or woman) is a sin against God, a defilement of the land, an offence against society and an act of wickedness against a fellow man.' 'And thine eye shall not have pity; but life shall go for life, eye for eye, tooth for tooth, hand for hand, foot for foot,' Deut 19:21.

In the twentieth century is it right to quote passages from the Bible as a justification for reintroducing something as barbaric as hanging? Write an essay explaining whether you are in favour of hanging or not and give reasons.

INFORMATION WAS OBTAINED FROM:

- The Police Federation of England and Wales. 15-17 Langley Road, Surbiton, Surrey KT6 6LP.
- Campaign for Law and Order. The Tower, Rainhill, Merseyside L35 6NE.
- Radical Alternatives to Prison. BCM Box 4852. London WC1N 3XX.
- NACRO. (National Association for the Care and Resettlement of Offenders). 169 Clapham Road, London SW9.
- Prison Officers Association. Cronin House, 245 Church Street, Edmonton, London N1 9HW.
- The Howard League for Penal Reform. 322 Kennington Park Road, London SE11 4PP.

CHAPTER 13

nuclear power

ASSIGNMENT ①

Look at the pictures titled *Nuclear Energy – Friend or Foe?* Discuss the uses and dangers of nuclear power.

Draw two columns and make a list of the uses and dangers of nuclear technology. Add to this list as you acquire more information.

NUCLEAR ENERGY - *FRIEND OR FOE*

Source: Hobson's Publishing plc

ASSIGNMENT ❷

Look at the passage *Risks*. Look at each paragraph carefully, discuss its meaning and then write down a few lines explaining what it is about and what it tells you about the benefits of nuclear power.

ASSIGNMENT ❸

Read *What Are The Alternatives?* and *The End of Nuclear Power* carefully.
Discuss in your groups what the viewpoints of the two writers are. Which do you believe the most?

Now work out exactly what each one says and how directly they say it. Both say some things directly and in great detail, some very indirectly without clearly stating their case. This very indirect way of saying things is called *implying* them. For example, *What Are the Alternatives?* says that nuclear energy 'could easily fill the gap until other energy sources

are developed.' This implies that other resources are running out but doesn't actually say so. *The End of Nuclear Power* says that 'Phasing out nuclear power and dealing responsibly with nuclear wastes, would be a major step forward to a safer, energy future.' This *implies* that nuclear power and waste are dangerous without actually saying so.

Draw up a table with the following headings.
Article A
States   **Implies**

Article B
States   **Implies**
and under each heading say how each article treats the following: *conventional fuels; alternatives to nuclear power; nuclear power.*

Discuss your views about the articles again. Have they changed? Which do you believe now? Write a brief paragraph based on your tables saying why you believe one article or the other.

RISKS

The risks of exposure to radiation command considerable public attention. However, few people realise that safety regulations governing the use of ionizing radiation and radioactive materials are generally stricter than those which apply to other potentially dangerous elements: radiation protection in fact sets an example to other safety disciplines.

In particular, the use of nuclear energy for electricity production is inevitably connected with the production of large amounts of radioactive materials that must and can be controlled. The major concerns of the nuclear industry are the prevention of accidents at power stations that might result in the release of large amounts of radioactive materials to the environment, and the long term isolation of radioactive wastes.

On the other hand, coal is and will remain for the foreseeable future a major contributor to energy supply. Burning coal for electricity production releases to the environment large quantities of sulphur dioxide, nitrogen oxides, and even some radioactivity (as a result of the presence of radium and other radioactive elements in coal). It gives rise as well to large volumes of fly ash which contain toxic metals. All fossil fuels produce carbon dioxide

when they are burned, and much concern has been expressed in recent years that increasing the proportion of carbon dioxide in the atmosphere could affect the world's climate. The use of other energy sources - even those which are apparently "benign", such as hydro-power - also gives rise to hazards. The risks and benefits of the use of any energy source on a large scale must therefore be carefully considered.

Benefits from the use of nuclear techniques in medicine, industry agriculture and other areas of scientific research, under carefully controlled conditions, clearly outweigh the risks. The uses of radiation have brought tremendous benefits to our everyday lives during the past 30 years, many of which are taken for granted. Radioactive elements - radioisotopes - and controlled radiation are used, for example, to sterilize medical supplies, to improve the keeping qualities of foodstuffs such as fruits and vegetables, spices and seasonings and some meat and fish products, in industrial processes and in medical science, in the study of the environment and of environmental pollution, in agriculture and in hydrology. Many of these uses are described in companion leaflets

available from the IAEA.

Medical diagnosis and treatment is the main source of public exposure to manmade radiation; the benefit of this exposure in terms of human lives saved is enormous. Radiation is a major tool in the treatment of certain kinds of cancer. Radioisotopes play an essential part in some medical diagnostic procedures: they are used for example in studies of the condition and functioning of body organs such as the heart, lung, brain, liver and kidney. Without radioisotopes, such studies would be difficult or impossible.

The use of gamma radiation to sterilize medical products such as syringes, surgical dressings, sutures, catheters and so on is now common. Many products of this sort are difficult to sterilize by heat or steam, and other sterilizing agents such as chemicals or gases may introduce undesirable residues. In addition, since the radiation penetrates the packing, items to be sterilized can be hermetically sealed before treatment. Since the use of radiation for sterilization is a "cold" process, it can be applied to heat sensitive materials such as plastics (in, for example, artificial valves for use in heart surgery). It appears to be the only means of sterilizing a number of heat-sensitive pharmaceutical items such as powders, ointments and solutions.

Source: International Atomic Energy Authority

WHAT ARE THE ALTERNATIVES?

COULD RENEWABLE ENERGY SOURCES SUPPLY OUR NEEDS?

Some only supply heat. Others could be used to generate electricity, but could they generate sufficient?

Power stations are rated in megawatts (MW); modern ones are normally 1000MW or 2000MW. (One megawatt will supply 1000 electric bar fires.)

To generate 1000MW you would need approximately

- *300 windmills on land or sea with rotors 100m across*
- *A large tidal barrier*
- *A very large dam for hydroelectric generation*
- *40 square kilometers of solar collector*
- *100 kilometers of ocean wave energy converters*
- *10 ocean thermal energy converters*
- *20,000 tonnes of biomass (plant crops or waste) per day*

Only the first four at present seem to be serious possibilities for Britain.

NUCLEAR ENERGY

Bear in mind, for comparison, that nuclear power stations:

- *cover the electrical base load reliably*
- *emit no sulphur dioxide which may cause acid rain*
- *are already developed and available*
- *could easily fill the gap until other energy sources are developed*

Source: UKAEA © Hobson's Publishing plc

THE END OF NUCLEAR POWER - TOWARDS A NEW BEGINNING

Phasing out nuclear power and dealing responsibly with nuclear wastes would be a major step forward to a safer energy future. But what about alternatives to the small amount of energy that nuclear power provides? To replace the 4% of our energy that comes from nuclear power, we can choose from many options:

❶ Improve Britain's energy conservation record, which is currently amongst the worst in Western Europe. This would save us all money, cutting down on waste which is currently costing us £7 billion per year, and creating thousands of jobs. Conservation particularly aimed at the electricity sector has the potential to save far more than the electricity currently provided by nuclear. A move towards more energy efficient fridges and freezers alone would save the equivalent of 2-3 Sizewell PWR's.

❷ Clean up the coal industry and improve its efficiency which would help solve the problems of acid rain. With 2-300 years supply of coal, we should plan how to use it cleanly and efficiently for the future by using the latest combustion technology and pollution control equipment.

❸ Many countries are now waking up to the potential of the renewable energy supplies. Renewable energy includes solar, tidal, wind, geothermal, biomass and wave energy. One British engineering firm recently won a £50 million contract to supply wind generators for California, whilst Norway has built a power station that takes energy from the waves using technology developed in Britain over the past 10 years. The potential for tidal energy, wind power, solar heating, geothermal heat and energy from biomass waste is immense. It has so far been starved of both funds and political commitment. Its Research and Development budget of £14 million per year contrasts sharply with the near £300 million per year provided for nuclear fission.

A non-nuclear energy future is not just a pipe-dream – many countries are already going down that path, such as Sweden, Denmark and Austria. It is not only possible, it is essential for our future survival and prosperity.

Source: Friends of the Earth

ASSIGNMENT ❹

Abnormally high leukaemia rate seen near Dounreay

CANCER STUDY POINTS FINGER AT ATOM PLANT
Rob Edwards

A Scottish nuclear power complex is the most likely cause of a higher than expected rate of leukaemia among children living nearby, government advisors said yesterday.

A report by the committee on Medical Aspects of Radiation in the Environment. CoMARE, said the evidence supported the hypothesis that some feature of the Dounreay works in Caithness increased the risk.

But it added: *"Conventional dose and risk estimates suggest that neither authorised nor accidental discharges could be responsible. There are however uncertainties about dose and risk calculations especially with respect to exposure of the foetus and small child."*

One committee member Dr Thomas Wheldon, insisted last night that in spite of all the caveats their conclusion was clear:*"On the balance of probabilities we think it is most likely that Dounreay and by implication Sellafield are to blame for the excesses of leukaemia."*

CoMARE was set up by the government in 1985 as a result of a recommendation by Sir Douglas Black's inquiry into high incidence of leukaemia round Sellafield, Cumbria, discovered by Yorkshire Television.

In the light of the nuclear industry's plans to build the world's largest plutonium re-processing works at Dounreay, the committee was asked to study the leukaemia excess there.

CoMARE points out that six cases of childhood leukaemia were registered round Dounreay between 1979 and 1984, when only one would have been expected. It says that the likelihood of that cluster happening by chance was very low.

It reveals three hitherto unknown leukaemia cases near Dounreay. Although there are difficulties in making comparisons these reinforce the committee's findings.

The committee also criticises Dounreay's operators, the UK Atomic Energy Authority, for the occasions on which radioactivity escaped from the works. Radioactive particles have been found on a public beach and on the seats of buses. In 1973, an error resulted in the discharge of strontium 90 to the sea exceeding the authorised limits for nine months.

"Though we have no expertise in this area," CoMARE says, *"this suggests to us that the safeguards against inadvertent transfer off site have not always been totally effective."*

The committee suggests various ways in which Dounreay might have increased the risk of leukaemia, emphasising the many uncertainties that govern risk estimates, especially to unborn children. It concludes that *"the evidence does not point to any particular explanation and therefore all possible explanations need to be investigated further"* and recommends a series of detailed studies of the leukaemia cases, increased monitoring particularly of people's diet, the air in population centres, sea spray and

sediments and a special survey of radioactivity in the dust of homes of the Dounreay leukaemia victims.

Whole-body monitoring and the measurement of radioactivity in placentae should take place near major nuclear installations, it says. The Scottish Office health minister, Michael Forsyth, said yesterday that the government accepted in principle all the recommendations.

The report will boost the campaign against the plan to build a European demonstration reprocessing works at Dounreay. The privatisation of electricity and the difficulties of international collaboration have already cast doubt over these plans, which were the subject of Scotland's longest public inquiry in 1986.

The UKAEA's chairman, Mr John Collier, said that although the report was a *"positive contribution"* to the debate, it was *"inconclusive"*. He rejected the implication that the staff may not have complied with the stringent safety procedures when leaving the site.

Dounreay's director Gerry Jordon said: *"Our overall cancer statistics in Caithness are good. We've one of the lowest rates in the whole country. That's why we're going to do all we can to help further investigation.*

But it is also why we are concerned that undue concentration on nuclear plants may hinder a search for the true causes of such a tragic but thankfully still rare disease."

Source: The Guardian 9/6/88

Read the article *Cancer Study Points Finger at Atom Plant.*

Look at paragraphs 1-4.

1 The Comare report found a higher than expected rate of leukaemia amongst children around the Dounreay nuclear power plant. What does it say probably causes this?

2 What do you think 'dose and risk estimates' are (paragraph 3)?

3 Does the committee think these estimates are reliable? Give reasons for your answer.

Look at paragraphs 5-8.

4 Why was Comare set up?

5 Why was it asked to investigate the Dounreay plant as well as the Sellafield plant?

6 If you lived near Dounreay what would your reaction be to the information in paragraphs 7 and 8?

Look at paragraphs 9-12.

7 Briefly describe why Comare think that safety procedures at Dounreay have not been satisfactory.

8 List the measures they say should be introduced next to find out more about leukaemia near major nuclear installations.

Look at paragraphs 13-15.

9 Who will welcome the report?

10 What did the UKAEA's chairman say about it?

11 What, if anything, did Dounreay's director say about leukaemia rates?

Whole article.

12 Are there any questions you would like to ask?

13 Is the headline appropriate? Would you change it and if so to what?

14 Having read this and the previous material about nuclear power, explain in a paragraph if you are in favour of it.

ASSIGNMENT 5

Imagine that you are a concerned parent who lives in the area around Dounreay. Write a letter to your local MP explaining how you feel about the results of the recent cancer study.

- As well as the health risks suggested by the study think of other dangers concerned with nuclear power.
- Make a careful list of the points you wish to mention in your letter.
- Remember that this should be set out as a formal letter.

ASSIGNMENT 6

Look at the picture of Albert Einstein and the accompanying quote. What do you think he meant?

Albert Einstein won a Nobel prize in 1921 for his work on relativity. Among other things, he made it possible to calculate just how much energy is released by nuclear fission with his famous equation: $E = MC^2$

Einstein once said about his work on nuclear energy:
"If only I had known, I should have become a watchmaker."
Do you think he was right to feel this way?

ASSIGNMENT 7

Read this letter to Professor Mathews together with *Man-made radiation* on page 124 and the information from Greenpeace and CND on pages 124–125.

Then conduct a radio interview in which Einstein explains why he is dismayed by the effects of the splitting of the atom.

23 March 1984

Management Advisory Committee,
Department of Applied Mathematics
and Theoretical Physics,
University of Cambridge,
Cambridge.

Dear Professor Matthews,
You don't know why I use 'out of date radiation levels', for God's sake I'm no nuclear scientist but I understand that No doubt you can come back at me with some nuclear nit-picking statistics. I don't care, I have no confidence in the nuclear industry radiation levels, I don't want my children exposed to any man-made radiation. Put it down to gut reaction, maternal instincts - these have not let me down in looking after my children and I don't want it
Good God, we've got on our doorstep what must be the most radioactive sea in the World - the Irish Sea - can you tell me of another sea which has 2.2 million gallons of water containing nuclear isotopes pumped into it daily?
Quite safe we've been told for years, now reductions must be made. So much for the levels?
Yes I'm angry, I make no apology, I cry with utter frustration that I cannot safeguard my children.

Yours sincerely

Deirdre Rhys-Thomas

- Decide carefully the questions you would ask.
- Refer to the uses we make of nuclear energy.

MAN-MADE RADIATION

Note 53: Professor Sadao Ichikawa, Professor of Genetics at Sainama University in Urawa, Japan, points out that man-made radiation is in fact more dangerous than natural radiation. It has been widely assumed that because man-made and natural radionuclides decay in the same way (by giving off gamma rays, and alpha or beta-particles with the same amount of energy) they would have the same health effects.

However, man-made radionuclides have a tendancy to accumulate in living tissues while natural ones do not. Ninety-nine per cent of internal exposure is due to potassium-40 which occurs abundantly in nature, but which moves through the tissues and organs of the body without building up. During the long history of evolution, plants or animals that did accumulate potassium-40 would have disappeared.

Some of the fission products of uranium such as **Iodine-131**, **Caesium-137** and **Strontium-90** (all of which were present in the Chernobyl cloud) concentrate in different organs; iodine in the thyroid, especially in young children, can be found at 3.5 to 10 million times the concentration in air. Once inside the body the accumulated doses of radiation can be extremely high for the surrounding tissues. **Caesium** is drawn to the organs of production, and can cause sterility or damaged gene cells.

It is therefore rather misleading to imply that because we have evolved in a radioactive world, a bit more won't do us any harm. The natural background radiation itself may well contribute to the onset of cancer and genetic defects. *See Ichikawa, Sadao. "Responses to Ionizing Radiation" in Encyclopedia of Plant Physiology, New Series, Volume 12A, Springer Verlag, Berlin, 1981.*

THE WORST KIND OF NUCLEAR ACCIDENT

The worst kind of accident at a nuclear plant would combine a breach of the reactor containment, a failure of the reactor's cooling systems and an uncontrollable fire within the reactor. These situations have already occurred at Chernobyl (USSR) where a reactor fire raged uncontrolled for six days before it was swamped by dumping tons of sand and boron onto it. At Windscale, the fire in 1957 vented radioactivity to the atmosphere through the reactor stack. The fire was eventually smothered by drenching the pile with water.

In graphite moderated thermal reactors, the risk of a chemical (hydrogen) explosion exists through a possible breach of a water pressure pipe venting steam or water onto the reactor's moderator.

A severe explosion could breach the reactor's containment system and destroy its cooling systems. In this case, whether a reactor fire becomes controllable or not depends on the severity of the structural damage, intensity of local radioactivity, the availability and willingness of adequately equipped fire fighting teams and many other imponderables. The Firemens Union in the UK has stated that there is no training or equipping of personnel to deal with nuclear graphite fires.

A severe and uncontrolled fire would almost certainly melt down the entire reactor core. At Chernobyl, it is estimated that 10% of the reactor's contents amounting to millions of curies of radioactivity, were vented into the atmosphere. At least one hundred thousand latent cancers will result from this contamination. In a worst case accident where the majority of the reactor's contents, including its plutonium, were to be released to the atmosphere, the consequences are very hard to estimate, but would certainly be catastrophic to life. On a crude basis, the number of immediate radiation deaths and long-term cancer rates would be a multiple of the proportion of reactor content released.ie. a 50% release could lead to 500 immediate deaths and 500,000 long-term cancers. Thousands, possibly hundreds of thousands of square miles of agricultural land would be dangerously irradiated and unsuitable for years.

What exactly happens at Sellafield?

The Sellafield nuclear fuel reprocessing plant is at the heart of Britain's civil and military nuclear complex. It is the dirtiest and most dangerous of all Britain's nuclear facilities. Using a chemical process, it separates the used fuel it receives from the British and foreign nuclear power stations into four main constituents: low and medium level radioactive waste; high-level radioactive waste; unused uranium fuel; and plutonium.

All the plutonium for Britain's warheads has at one stage or another passed through the plant. Under cross examination by CND at the Sizewell Inquiry, BNFL admitted that it 'co-processes' fuel from the military reactors at Calder Hall and Chapelcross with fuel from the civil electricity board reactors. If reprocessing did not take place the waste disposal problem would be eased and the supply of plutonium for weapons would eventually run out. There is also a secret 'plutonium recoveries' facility at Sellafield which is probably used to treat plutonium in ageing nuclear warheads.

Source: CND

What about the problems of nuclear waste?

After three decades of nuclear power, the British nuclear industry - civil and military - still has no clear idea of how it will dispose of its radioactive waste. High-level waste, which remains dangerous for centuries, is stored above ground at the Sellafield pending a decision on how to dispose of it. Having been prevented from dumping at sea by the trade unions, the industry is desperately looking for new dumping sites for low and medium level waste. The government nuclear waste organisation, NIREX, has encountered fierce opposition to its attempts to investigate four potential low level dumps - at Fulbeck in Lincolnshire, Bradwell in Essex, Killingholme on Humberside and Elstow in Bedfordshire.

Source: CND

ASSIGNMENT ⑧

Read the article *Radiation Is All Around Us* and the advertisements *The CEGB Proves Its Point*, and *Diesel No. 46009's Last Run* on page 126.

As a group prepare a talk by an employee of the Central Electricity Generating Board. The employee is promoting a plan to build a nuclear reactor plant in your area.

- Remember that this talk should be persuasive.
- Think carefully about the type of language you would use.
- How would you make this idea seem attractive to the inhabitants of the area?
- What could you offer them?
- What about the safety aspects?

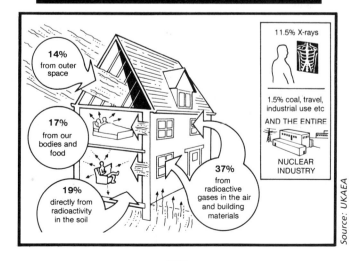

Radiation is all around us

14% from outer space

17% from our bodies and food

19% directly from radioactivity in the soil

37% from radioactive gases in the air and building materials

11.5% X-rays

1.5% coal, travel, industrial use etc

AND THE ENTIRE NUCLEAR INDUSTRY

Source: UKAEA

THE CEGB PROVES ITS POINT

In the mid-summer of 1984 a worldwide television audience of millions watched as a diesel train travelling at 100 mph crashed into a nuclear fuel flask.

The diesel was destroyed.

The flask – carrying steel rods to simulate nuclear fuel – was unscathed.

The Central Electricity Generating Board – which organised the demonstration to show its total confidence in the immense strength of these containers – had proved its point.

DIESEL NO. 46009'S LAST RUN

The locomotive used in the nuclear fuel flask train crash was number 46009. It had been withdrawn from service early in 1984 after 22 years of handling passenger and freight traffic and was due to be scrapped.

The locomotive weighed 140.5 tonnes – the heaviest type used on British Rail's network.

The 3 coaches used were Mark 1 stock recently withdrawn from service. They were built in 1951 and each weighed 35 tonnes.

At Edwalton, in Nottinghamshire an engineer threw a switch to start the train. It accelerated to 100 mph over about 8 miles of track – an impact speed more than equalling the peak force exerted by a High Speed Train at 125 mph.

At Old Dalby in Leicestershire the train struck the nuclear fuel flask on the lid as it lay on the track in the cradle of a derailed flatrol – the worst imaginable position.

The crash was spectacular – a devastating explosion of flame and fire.

It took 5 seconds for all components involved in the crash to come to rest.

The locomotive was crushed. The carriages were badly damaged.

But the point of the demonstration had been made – the nuclear fuel flask was completely intact.

Source: Central Electricity Board National Power Division.

ASSIGNMENT ⑨

Review the material that you have been given.

Do the two sides present their material differently? Which is more easily readable and more visual?

Why might this be?

Could some of the organisations opposed to nuclear power afford to crash a locomotive to prove a point?

What does this tell you?
Try to distinguish what is being said from the way it is presented.

Decide as a group whether you are in favour of nuclear power or not.

ASSIGNMENT ⑩

It has been decided that a nuclear power station is to be built near your town. Attempt all of the following written assignments.

1 Write a newspaper article for a local paper that highlights the benefits to the area of a nuclear plant or highlights the dangers.
2 Write a letter to the paper opposing the point of view put forward by the reporter.
3 Imagine that you work for an advertising agency that has been approached by the CEGB. They want you to design an advertisement for peak time television viewing. Explain in detail the advertisement you would make. You could draw a story board to illustrate your ideas.
4 Design a wall advertisement in opposition to the plant and commissioned by Greenpeace.
5 A public debate is to be held to discuss the siting of the plant. Script the discussion that could take place between residents, supporters of environmental groups and the CEGB. Each group should voice its opinions with reasons. This could be an oral piece of work instead of a written piece with groups representing various interested parties.

The interested parties would be:
People who wish to obtain jobs in the industry.
Parents of young children and pregnant mothers.
Official of the CEGB.
Members of Green groups, and so on.

INFORMATION WAS OBTAINED FROM:

- The Central Electricity Generating Board. Dept. of Information and Public Affairs, Sudbury House, 15 Newgate Street, London EC1A 7AU
- National Radiological Protection Board. Chiltern, Didcot, Oxon OX11 0RQ
- Friends of the Earth Trust Ltd. 377 City Road, London EC1V 1NA.
- Greenpeace. 30-31 Islington Green, London N1 8XE.
- UK Atomic Energy Authority. AEA Education Service, Oxfordshire OX11 0RA.

Acknowledgements

The author and publisher would like to thank the following for permission to reproduce copyright material:

A & M Records Inc for the lyrics of 'Children's Crusade by Sting from *Dream of the Blue Turtle*; *Angler's Mail* for 'Get It Over Quickly' 19/3/88; Animal Aid for the posters 'Porion Down Torture Town', 'Painkillers Are Banned' and 'Human Hunger'; ASH (Action on Smoking and Health) for 'Advertising Agreement Failing to Protect Children'; The British Fur Trade Association for 'The Fascinating World of Fur'; CAA (Campaign for the Abolition of Angling) for the poster 'Angling the Neglected Bloodsport'; The Campaign for Law and Order for 'Another Powerful Argument'; The Canadian Broadcasting Corporation for the poem by Margaret Atwood from *Poems for Voices*: The Central Electricity Board National Power Division for 'The CEGB Proves Its Point'; CND (The Campaign for Nuclear Disarmament) for the articles 'Deadly Myths', 'What Exactly Happens at Sellafield' and the article on p. 35. Compassion in World Farming for 'Born To Be Flayed' and 'Let the Frogs Keep Their Legs'; *Course Angler Magazine* for 'Anglers Raise 15,000 for Cancer Research (Vol. 111 no. 6, Nov. 1987); *The Daily Express* for 'Nessie: Sonar and Yet So Far' 10/10/87; *The Daily Mail* for 'No You Can't Walk Out On A Poltegeist' 14/4/88; *The Daily Mirror* for 'Act for Children' cartoons from *The London Daily News*; *The Daily Star* for I Invented Yeti . . .' 27/10/88; *The Daily Telegraph* and Peter Gilman for 'An Abominable Saga Unfolds' 12/6/86; Judy Daish Associates Ltd for the extract from 'Whose Life Is It Anyway?' by Brian Clark, © Brian Clark 1978 (Amber Lane Press 1978); Faber and Faber Limited for the poem 'Colobus Monkey' (translated from the Yoruba by Uli Beier) from *The Rattle Bag*, ed Heaney/Hughes; FOREST (The Freedom Association for the Right to Enjoy Smoking Tobacco) for the pro-smoking sticker and 'Carry On With the Sport'; *The Globe and Mail* for 'Destruction of a Seal Market'; Greenpeace for 'The Worst Kind of Nuclear Accident'; *The Guardian* and Derek Morgan for 'Fags Dragged Into Court' 20/7/88, and Rob Edwards for 'Cancer Study Points Finger Atom Plant' 9/6/88; *Guernsey Evening Press* for 'Smokers's Campaigner Fights to Keep Liberty and Balance'; Hamish Hamilton for the extract from *When the Wind Blows* by Raymond Briggs © 1982 Raymond Briggs; *The Health Education Journal* for 'A Representative Survey'; Hobsons Publishing PLC for 'Who Protects the Animals?', 'Nuclear Energy: Friend or Foe?' and 'What are the Alternatives?'; The International Atomic Energy Agency for 'Risks – Radiation – A Fact of Life'; *The Liverpool Daily Post* for 'Know-alls'; *The Liverpool Echo* for 'Smokers Unite'; LYNX for the posters 'How would You Like Your Fur, Madam?', 'It takes up to 40 animals to . . .', 'Witness to a Killing' and 'Help Us Get the Fur Trade Off the Nation's Back; Macmillan Magazines Ltd for 'Naming the Loch Ness Monster' from *Nature* Vol. 258 11/12/75; *The Mail on Sunday* for 'Did I See the Yeti?' 22/5/88 and 'Stop This Act of Folly' 16/10/88; NACRO (National Campaign for the Care and Resettlement of Offenders) for 'Terrorism'; The National Federation of Anglers for 'Anglers and Conservation', 'Take A Friend Fishing' and 'How Anglers Protect the Environment'; NAVS for 'Warfare experiments' The Norfolk Anglers Conservation Association for Angling In Touch With Nature'; Northwest Territories Renewable Sources for 'A Special Message'; *The Observer* for 'A Baby's Right To Live or Die' 16/8/81; Oxfam and Ian Kellas for the cartoons on p. 107; Peace Through Nato for the article and photographs on p. 35 and for 'Non-threatening Deterrant' and 'Which Way'; *The People* and Chris Bofey for 'Cats Tortured To Find A Cure for Backache'; Peters Fraser & Dunlop Group Ltd for the poem 'Icarus Allsorts' by Roger McGough from *The Mersey Sound*; *Pisces* for 'Just Because the Fish Don't Scream Doesn't Mean It's Not Murder', 'Waterways Users Condemn Anglers' and 'Fish Farmer Fined' (April/June 1988); The Police Federation of England and Wales for the article on p. 116; John Pudney for the poem 'Ballad of the Long Drop' © John Pudney; Punch Publications Ltd for the cartoons 'Smokeless Zones'; The Research Defense Society for 'For All Our Sakes Science Still Needs Animals'; The RSPCA (The Royal Society for the Prevention of Cruelty to Animals') for 'Fur and the Fury'; Vernon Scannell for the poem 'Incendiary'; SPUC (The Society for the Protection of Unborn Children) for the advertisement on p. 64; Secker & Warburg Ltd for 'A Hanging, Adelphi 1931' by George Orwell; *The Sunday Telegraph* and Violet Johnstone for 'Teaching the Sins of the Flesh' 1/11/87; *The Sunday Times* and Dr Colin Brewer for 'Worse Than Death' 18/9/84; *The Times* for the cartoon by Barry Fantoni © Times Newspapers Ltd, and the article 'Nato's Armies Lag Behind the Eastern Block' 19/10/88 © Times Newspapers Ltd 1988; and Heather Kirby for the article 'One Child's Meat 25/2/88'; *TODAY* for 'Stripped of Gold' 27/9/88, 'Shut Smokers Away In Corner' 23/3/88, 'Smoking Yob Extinguished . . .' 27/9/88, 'Softly, softly . . .' 30/9/88, 'Bribe Them With A New Car' 30/9/88; 'Nine Reasons Why the Weed Wins', 30/9/88' 'Three Out of Four Back Mercy Killing' 24/3/88, 'Women Speak With One Voice' 22/9/88; Unwin Hyman Ltd for the extract from *Letters for My Children* by Deirdre Rhys Thomas; The Vegetarian Society for 'Put Less of Your Money Where Your Mouth Is' and 'By the time you've finished reading this article 50 animals have been slaughtered for food' and 'The World Holds Enough for Every Man's Need . . .'; The Vegan Society for 'World Tragedy; 30 Jumbo Jet Crashes Every Day'; Warner Chappell Music Ltd for 'Don't Ban the Bomb' by Rod McKuen from *Rod Mckuen at Carnegie Hall*, and for the lyrics from *Ghostbusters* © 1984 Golden Torch Music/Raydida Music.

It has not been possible to trace all copyright holders. The publisher would be glad to hear from any unacknowledged sources at the first opportunity.

The author and publisher would also like to thank the following for permission to reproduce photographs on the pages indicated:

J. Allan Cash Ltd, p. 76 left; Barnaby's Picture Library, p. 76 right; Jane Bown (Observer) p. 67; Central Electricity Generating Board, p. 121; Rene Dahinden/Fortean Picture Library p. 72; Express Newspapers, p. 47; Fortean Picture Library, p. 97 top and bottom left; Melvin Grey/NHPA, p. 85; Hiroshima/Nagasaki Publishing Committee, p.19 bottom left; Imperial War Museum, p. 19 bottom right, p. 37; Dr Ian Johnson, p. 50; Philippe Plailly/Science Photo Library, p. 121; Syndication International Ltd, p. 97 bottom right; Times Newspapers Ltd, p. 104; US National Archives/Science Photo Library, p. 19 top; R. K. Wilson/Fortean Picture Library, p. 45.